the Ultimate Conspiracy

Milan Martin

The Ultimate Conspiracy

Milan Martin Ministries
P.O. Box 702741
Tulsa, Oklahoma 74170-2741
www.milanmartinministriesinc.com

ISBN 9780997612424

Printed in the United States of America

Table of Contents

Chapter 1- The Preadamit World 7

Chapter 2- The Seed of the Woman 23

Chapter 3- The Counterfeit Seed 37

Chapter 4- The Ancient Book of Jasher 55

Chapter 5- The Ancient Book of Enoch...................................... 63

Chapter 6- The Roots of Paganism... 71

Chapter 7- The roots of Witchcraft 79

Chapter 8-The Abrahamic Covenant 87

Chapter 9- The promised Seed.. 99

Chapter 10- The Pentecostal Church 107

Chapter 11- Seven Feasts for Israel... 119

Chapter 12- America's Pagan Capital 135

Chapter 13- The Sun clothed Woman 153

Chapter 14- Victorious Church Vision. 165

Front Cover

On the front cover is a depiction of what some call the Goat of Mendes, or the Baphomet, created by the French Luciferian Eliphas Levi. Levi is often referred to as the Michelangelo of Black Magic because of his engraving of the Knight Templars idle, which they called the Baphomet.

Back Cover

Featured on the back cover of this book is a nineteen foot tall bronze statue of Semiramis, the wife of the biblical Nimrod. Semiramis today sets atop America's Capital Building, which is located just across from the obelisk known as the Washington Monument. This obelisk was built by the Freemasons to represent Nimrod's erect phallus. The rotunda inside our Capital Building was designed by the Freemasons to represent the pregnant belly and womb of Nimrod's wife Semiramis. The eminent Masonic scholar Manly P Hall, wrote in his book *The Secret Teachings of All Ages:* **"The Dying God** (Nimrod/Osiris) **shall rise again! The secret room in the House of the Hidden Places shall be rediscovered. The Pyramid again shall stand as the ideal emblem of resurrection, and regeneration."** The Freemasons believe after Nimrods death, he was buried inside the Great Pyramid at Giza, where he is now patiently awaiting his resurrection and regeneration. The Freemasons arranged to have this Pyramid, with the eye of Nimrod/Osiris atop it, placed on the back of our one-dollar bills, as a representation of this belief.

Introduction

Starting in the *Book of Genesis,* and running throughout the entire *Old Testament* we are given brief glances of a rebellion to God's authority which involved a full third of the angels of heaven. This rebellion was led by a mysteriously beautiful, and wise creature known as Lucifer, which God had given much power and authority to administer over his heavenly mercy seat. This heavenly rebel is called by several names throughout the *New Testament,* but Jesus usually referred to him as the Devil, or Satan. When one considers the magnitude of this rebellion, and the spiritual ramifications it has had on all of God's creation, it is a wonder that so little is said about Lucifer in the *Bible.* This rebellion took place long before the creation of Adam and Eve, for Lucifer was already labeled a spiritual outlaw long before the six days of creation listed in the book of *Genesis.* In this book I shall try to relate to the reader, in a simple way, some of the details of a mysterious plan the godhead devised. God the Father, God the Son, and God the Holy Spirit secretly conspired together among themselves to legally deal with Lucifer's universal rebellion. The godhead then chose to keep this plan a secret even from his faithful angels, thus we have a mystery that involves a "Promised Seed" that runs throughout the *Bible.* Although some theologians have labeled this mystery "the plan of redemption," I prefer to think of it as "God's Ultimate Conspiracy." The details of this divinely inspired plan would be hidden from everybody, including Lucifer, for God was careful not to tell him too much. May God now grant you the reader eyes to see this mysterious plan which has been hidden from all but God's elect from the foundation of the earth?

Dedication

Dedicated to my best friend and wife Reva, who has loyally stood by my side through fifty years of both the best of times, and the worst of times. Without her prayers and dedication to my wellbeing, and ministry, and her constant collaboration with me, this book would never have been possible.

Chapter I

The Preadamite World

As stated in the introduction of this book, God the father, God the son, and God the Holy Spirit are at this very moment in time dealing with a spiritual outlaw, a spiritual thief who is determined to steal away God's authority over his own creation. Being a just God, he must deal with this spiritual rebel, and his fallen angelic followers in such a way that is in line with his own since of fairness and justice. God has chosen to create mankind as free moral agents free to choose who they will serve, love and worship. The angels also were given this choice and unfortunately a third of them chose to love, worship, and serve Lucifer. When we consider that mankind, as well as the angels were both created by a loving god, we can understand the dilemma God was in between his since of love, and his since of justice. Lucifer would love nothing more than to have all of mankind to worship him rather than the creator, which is apparently what happened in the Preasamite World. Thus, after the creation of Adam and Eve, a conspiracy was once again devised between Lucifer and his fallen angels to deceive and steal away mankind's God given dominion and authority over this earth. Unlike in the Preadamite World where Lucifer had a God given dominion over the earth, today Lucifer has no legal authority in this earth-age over Christians except for the authority we give him through sin, deception and ignorance of God's word. Lucifer can do nothing in this earth without a physical body, thus to accomplish his goals in this earth-age he deceives and motivates mankind to act in his behalf. In order to deal with this spiritual rebel, God the Father, God the Son, and God the Holy Spirit devised a secret counter-conspiracy in order to rescue mankind from this spiritual outlaw. As stated in the introduction of this book I choose to refer to this secret counter-conspiracy as God's Ultimate Conspiracy. God not only chose to hide the details of this counter-conspiracy from Lucifer, but from his own faithful angels also (see *I Peter 1:12*), thus they long to better understand it. There are no details given to us in the *Bible* as to when Lucifer was first created, for God has not chosen to reveal all the mysteries of creation to us. Theologians often refer to this mysterious period of time by such terms as the Antediluvian World, the Anti-Chaotic Age, and the Dispensation of Angels, which included Lucifer. Throughout history Lucifer was often worshiped as both the Sun-God, and the Moon-God, and called by many pagan names such as Allah, Pan, Mephistopheles, Anubis, Bacchus, Orion, Draco, Jahbulon, San, Shamas, Amman, Enki, Ea, Ra, Raw, Tammuz, Horus, Osiris, Thoth, Tat, Kadmus, Adad, Saturn, Bel, Baal, Ball. Moloch, Tophet, Marduk, Murdoc, Milcom, Hadad, Pazuzu, Pan, Fazuzu, Adramelech, Anamelch, Mithras, Zeus, Zernebogus, Apollo, Sheikh, Shems, Nebo, Nito, Belial, Beelzebul, Beelzebub, and Satan. We know that Lucifer was already a fallen creature long before he seduced Eve in the Garden of Eden. The *Bible* plainly teaches that it has been about six thousand years since the creation of Adam and Eve, but we are not told exactly how old the earth really is. We know that Lucifer, on various occasions, before his fall appeared before God's throne, when all the stars, or angels of God were gathered together. After the creation of the earth, God told Job that all the morning stars, and all the sons of God, including Lucifer, celebrated and sang together celebrating the creation of the earth. "**Where was thou (Job) when I laid the foundations of the earth? Declare, if thou hast understanding. Who hath laid the measures thereof, if thou knowest? Or who hath stretched the line upon it? Whereupon are the foundations thereof fastened? Or who laid the corner stone thereof; when the morning stars sang together, and all the sons of God shouted for joy.**" *Job 38:4-7*

The term "sons of God" is used eight times in the *Old Testament* and in all eight incidences it refers to angels. Lucifer was no doubt present at this celebration because one of his titles is The Morning Star. It must be understood that the *Bible* teaches that Satan, the Devil, Beelzebub, Belial, Son of the Morning, Great Dragon, Old Serpent and Morning Star are all names that clearly refer to Lucifer. The following scripture includes four of these names. "**And his (Lucifer's) tail drew the third part of the stars (angels) of heaven. And the great dragon was cast out, that old serpent, called the Devil, and Satan, which deceived the whole world: he was cast out into the earth, and his angels were cast out with him.**" *Revelation 12:4-9*

If Lucifer was already a fallen being before the creation of Adam and Eve, his fall must have happened at a much earlier time. If Adam and Eve were created only about six thousand years ago, then how old is the earth? Many *Bible*-believing Christians may be surprised to hear the answer is not just thousands, but, according to scientists, possibly millions of years old. As a former pastor, I am often amazed at the astonished looks I get when making such a statement. Before you write my statement off as heresy, let us review a few scriptures you may never have studied closely before. **"They that see thee (Lucifer) shall narrowly look upon thee, and consider thee saying, is this the man that made the earth to tremble, that did shake kingdoms; that made the world as a wilderness, and destroyed the cities thereof; that opened not the house of his prisoners?"** *Isaiah 14:16-17*

Please note the context of this scripture plainly shows that God is addressing Lucifer **after** he had made the earth to tremble and become as a wilderness, and **after** he had destroyed cities, and weakened the nations. (**How art thou fallen from heaven O Lucifer, son of the morning! how art thou cut down to the ground, which did weaken the nations!**) *Isaiah: 12-12*

For purposes of clarity, let me ask once again, when did Lucifer shake kingdoms and make the earth to tremble? When did Lucifer make the world as a wilderness, and when did he destroy cities and take prisoners? There is no record in the *Bible* of Lucifer or Satan doing such things after the creation of Adam and Eve, thus we are left to conclude that it could only have happened before there creation. The prophet Ezekiel confirms Lucifer's first destructive career when he tells us that Lucifer had defiled his sanctuaries. In the context of this prophecy, God at first is speaking to the "Prince of Tyrus," but it is clear God's focus quickly shifts to Lucifer: **"Thou (Lucifer) hast defiled thy sanctuaries by the multitude of thine iniquities, by the iniquity of thy traffic; therefore will I bring forth a fire from the midst of thee, it shall devour thee, and I will bring thee to ashes upon the earth in the sight of all them that behold thee."** *Ezekiel 28: 18*

The end result of the judgement upon the Preadamite World was the destruction of all of mankind, and the earth being completely covered with both water and darkness. The prophet Jeremiah pointed to this same darkness in which there was no man, and also a great earthquake, when he said: **"I beheld the earth, and lo, it was without form** (tohu-disturbed), **and void** (bohu-empty); **and the heavens, and they had no light. I beheld the mountains, and, lo, they trembled, and all the hills moved lightly. I beheld, and, lo, there was no man, and all the birds of the heavens were fled. I beheld, and lo, the fruitful place was a wilderness, and all the** cities thereof were broken down at the presence of the Lord, and by his fierce anger." *Jeremiah 4:23-26*

The prophet Jeremiah went on to say: "For thus hath the Lord said, the whole land shall be desolate; yet will I not make a full end. For this shall the earth morn, and "the heavens above be black: because I have spoken it, I have purposed it, and will not repent, neither will I turn back from it." *Jeremiah 4:27-28*

In the *New Testament* the Apostle Peter refers to this same Preadamite flood when he said: "For this they willingly are ignorant of, that by the word of God the heavens were of old, and the earth standing out of the water: Whereby the world that then was, being overflowed with water, perished; But the heavens and the earth, which are now, by the same word are kept in store, reserved unto fire against the day of judgement and perdition of ungodly men." *II Peter 3:5-7*

The Psalmist also indicates that thousands of years ago man was destroyed by a flood. Was this Noah's flood, or was he speaking of a much earlier flood, far older than Adam and Eve, or Noah? Was there two floods? Again the Psalmist indicates that there were two floods when stating: "Thy throne is established of old: thou art from everlasting. The floods have lifted up, O Lord, the floods have lifted up their voice; the floods lift up their waves." *Psalms 93: 2-3*

If these were the only scripture in the *Bible* to prove there were two floods, I would be on shaky ground, but there are others. Again the Psalmist sheds further light when he said: "Who laid the foundations of the earth, that it should not be removed forever. Thou coverest it with the deep as with a garment: the waters stood above the mountains. At thy rebuke they fled; at the voice of thy thunder they hasted away. They go up by the mountains; they go down by the valleys unto the place which thou hast founded for them. Thou hast set a bound that they may not pass over; that they turn not again to cover the earth." *Psalms 104:5-9*

At first this scripture looks to be a reference to Noah's flood, but there are differences. Noah's flood took a year and seventeen days to dry up, but the waters of this flood hastened away at Gods thunderous rebuke, quickly returning to the bowels of the earth. We have conformation of this flood in the New Testament also.

The *Bible* tells us that there were six days of recreation, but on the Seventh day God rested. We know from the genealogical records of the *Bible* that Adam and Eve were created about six thousand years ago, but is the earth only that old? *Bible* scholars have wrestled with this question for years, and some have come up with what they often call the gap theory. I personally believe at least some of the gap theory to be true and will do my best in this small book to present this theory to you in a simple and understandable way, and let you come to your own conclusions. The prophet Ezekiel tells us that Lucifer was an angel of the cherub class who covered, or had authority over the throne of God. He was of the highest class of the angels until iniquity was found in him because of his great beauty, wisdom, and brightness. **"Thou sealest up the sum, full of wisdom, and perfect in beauty. Thou hast been in Eden the garden of God; every precious stone was thy covering."** Ezekiel continues: **The workmanship of thy tabrets and thy pipes was prepared in the in the day that thou wast created. Thou art the anointed cherub that covereth; and I have set thee so: thou wast upon the holy mountain of God; thou hast walked up and down in the midst of the stones of fire. Thou wast perfect in thy ways from the day that thou wast created, till iniquity was found in thee."** *Ezekiel 28:12-15*

Ezekiel goes on to inform us that Lucifer, because of his beauty, defiled himself by pride, which got him removed from the Mountain of God, where God's throne is located. **"By the multitude of thy merchandise they have filled the midst of thee with violence, and thou hast sinned: therefore I will cast thee as profane out of the mountain of God: and I will destroy thee O covering cherub, from the midst of the stones of fire. Thine heart was lifted up because of thy beauty, thou hast corrupted thy wisdom by reason of thy brightness: I will cast thee to the ground, I will lay thee before kings, that they may behold thee."** *Ezekiel 28: 16-17*

Even though Lucifer was created by God, the prophet Isaiah tells us that because of pride he was cast to the earth because he desired to be equal with God. **"How art thou fallen from heaven, O Lucifer, son of the morning? How art thou cut down to the ground, which didst weaken the nations? For thou hast said in thine heart, I will ascend into the heaven, I will exalt my throne above the stars of God: I will sit also upon the mount of the congregation, in the sides of the north: I will ascend above the heights of the clouds; I will be like the most High. Yet thou shall be**

brought down to hell, to the sides of the pit." *Isaiah 14:12-15*

After the fall of Lucifer, which means bringer of light or light bearer, the *Bible* almost always refers to him by the name Satan which is a military term meaning enemy or adversary, or by the name Devil (diabolos), which means slanderer or accuser. Because so many Christians have little or no knowledge of the Preadamite World, for purposes of clarity, I will repeat what I have said earlier in this chapter in a different way using the term gap theory. Again those of us who hold to the gap theory believe Lucifer once ruled over a world populated by people long before the creation of Adam and Eve. In the scriptures we have just reviewed we see Lucifer corrupting an entire world-system because of his pride, and his desire to be equal with God. Lucifer corrupted this first world-system, or Predamite World which brought on the judgement of God, just as he would later corrupt the people of Noah's day, and again bring on the judgement of God. In the book of *Genesis* we read that God created the heavens and the earth, and those of us who believe in the gap theory holds to the belief that there is a considerable chaotic gap of time between verse one, and verse two of the first chapter of *Genesis*. **"In the beginning** (reshiyth-on the first day of Tishri) **God** (Elohim-Gods) **created** (Bara-to make something from nothing) **the heaven** (shamayim-higher heaven, or constellations) **and the earth.** (folowed by a considerable chaotic gap of time) **And the earth** (erets-dry land) **was** (hayah-became) **without form** (tohuw-disrupted), **and void** (bohuw-empty); **and darkness** (choshek-unnatural darkness) **was upon the face of the deep** (tehowm-abyss). **And the spirit of God moved** (rachaph-pondered while moving) **upon the face of the waters."** *Genesis 1:1-2*

In other words in the beginning the godhead created the constellations and the earth from non-existing material and gave Lucifer dominion over the earth. When Lucifer was later judged for his pride the dry land of the earth became devoid of life and was covered with water and with supernatural darkness. After a considerable period of time the Spirit of God moved over the earth considering how to restore it to a habitable state. For purposes of clarity let me say again in a different way, I believe in the beginning God placed Lucifer over a pristine and populated world. Because of his pride Lucifer perverted and defiled this world, thus it was destroyed by an earthquake and flood. I further believe verse two of Genesis chapter one, describes a ruined and dark world which, at first was pristine, but then its cities were destroyed and became without form and void of life. In this judgment, darkness covered the Preadamite earth, causing all forms of life to quickly die, both in the oceans, and upon the earth. Imagine, without the rays of the sun, how cold the earth would become within a very short period of time. Referring to this calamity, author G. H. Pember, in his book *Earths Earliest Ages* states: **"Violent convulsions must have taken place upon it (the earth), for it was inundated with the ocean waters. Its sun had been extinguished, the stars were no longer seen above it. Its clouds and atmosphere, having no attractive force to keep them in suspension, had descended in moisture upon its surface. There was not a living being to be found in the whole planet."** This ruined, dark, and flooded earth, with its destroyed cities was in need of being recreated if God was to restore and repopulate the earth with mankind. The six days of creation spoken of in the remainder of the first and second chapters of *Genesis* is in reality a recreation, or restored earth, capable of once again sustaining life. Let me say again, the six days of creation was part of a recreation, or repopulation of plants and animals upon the earth so that Adam and Eve could later be given dominion over them. Adam was created (asah-to make something from existing material) form the red clay of the earth, and Eve was later created (asah-from the body of Adam). Adam was first formed (yatzar-to mold with the hand) from the red clay of the earth, while Eve was formed (yatzar) by the hand of God from Adam's side. Adam and Eve were placed in a garden planted east of Eden, which was probably located somewhere within the bourders of the modern country of Irock. God created the material universe to be inhabited with intelligent, free moral agents, to whom he could commune and reveal himself to. In verse two of the first chapter of *Genesis*, we find an additional Hebrew word which shines further light on the subject of the gap theory. **"And the earth was without form, and void; and darkness was upon the face of the deep. And the spirit of God moved** (rachaph-brooded or pondered) **upon the face of the waters."** *Genesis 1:2*

Said in a slightly different way, in the beginning of the Pre-Adamite world God did not create the world in a tohuw or bohuw, ruined and empty condition, but rather it hayah (became) that way after Lucifer's rebellion, followed by God's judgment. We have confirmation of this when Isaiah tells us that God did not originally create the earth without form and void, but rather it was created ready to be inhabited. **"For thus saith the Lord that created the heavens; God himself that formed** (yatsar-handmade)

the earth and made it, he hath established (kuwn-firmly erected) **it, he created it not in vain** (tohuw-destroyed), **he formed** (yatsar-handmade) **it to be inhabited."** *Isaiah 45:18*

In 1977 my family and I moved from Tulsa, Oklahoma to Dallas, Texas, so that I could attend Christ for the Nations Bible College. Later, while attending North Dallas Community Church, I taught a Bible study in which I mentioned the Preadamite world, and the possibility that man and dinosaurs might have once walked this earth together. Knowing little about Texas, I was astonished when I was told of two places in Texas where proof of what I had just said might be seen. The next Saturday morning my family and I headed out to Dinosaur State Park, in Glenrose, Texas. There, in the petrified rocks, human foot prints can be seen walking across dinosaur tracks. I was then told similar tracts could be seen at Thayer's Museum, at Dinosaur Flats in Canyon Lake, Texas. In the Preadamite World, God made a perfect earth, ready to be inhabited, but in the six day recreation, Adam and Eve's earth had to be refurbished before it could be repopulated and inhabited.

On day one of this recreation God started refurbishing the earth by rebuking both the waters and the darkness covering the earth which allowed sunlight to again penetrate the dense cloud cover surrounding the earth. God then divided the light from the darkness, calling the light day, and the darkness night. **"And God said, let there be** (allow permission to become) **light: and there was** (became) **light. And God saw the light, that it was good: and God divided the light from the darkness. And God called the light day, and the darkness he called night. And the evening and the morning were the first day."** *Genesis 1:1-5*

The Book of Jubilees is not a translation of the *Bible,* thus it is not considered to be inspired by God, but it does provide for us an additional historical account of the six days of creation. *The Book of Jubilees* states: **"For on the first day He created the heavens which are above and the earth and waters and all the spirits which serve before him. The angels of the presence, and the angels of sanctification, and the angels of the spirit of fire and the angels of the spirit of the winds, and the angels of the spirit of the clouds, and of darkness, and of snow and of hail and of hoar frost, and the angels of the voices and of the thunder and of the lightning, and the angel of the spirits of the cold and of heat, and of** winter and of spring and of autumn and of summer and of all the spirits of his creatures which are in the heavens and on the earth. He created the abysses and the darkness, eventide and night, and the light, dawn and day, which he hath prepared in the knowledge of his heart. And thereupon we saw His works, and praised Him, and lauded before Him on account of all His works; for seven great works did He create on the first day." *Jubilees 2:2-3*

The Septuagint is a Greek translation of the Hebrew *Old Testament,* created for the Jews who knew Koine Greek. *The Septuagint* states: "**In the beginning God made the heaven and earth. But the earth was unsightly and unfinished, and darkness was over the deep, and the Spirit of God moved over the water. And God said, Let there be light, and there was light. And God saw the light that it was good, and God divided between the light and the darkness. And God called the light Day, and the darkness he called Night, and there was evening and there was morning, the first day.**" *Genesis 1:1-5*

On day two of the recreation, God refurbished the firmament, or clouds, by dividing the waters that had formerly been in suspension over the clouds, which was the firmament, from the waters under the clouds which then covered the earth. In other words, the sunlight which had formerly evaporated water into our earthly heavens, after being darkened could no longer hold this same water in suspension, thus resulting in a world-wide flood. "**And God said, let there be a firmament** (raqia-extended firm surface) **in the midst of the waters, and let it divide the waters from the waters. And God made the firmament, and divided the waters which were under the firmament from the waters which were above the firmament: and it was so. And God called the firmament Heaven. And the evening and the morning were the second day.** " *Genesis 1:6-8*

The Book of Jubilees states: "**And on the second day He created the firmament in the midst of the waters, and the waters were divided on that day, half of them went up above, and half of them went down below the firmament that was in the midst over the face of the whole earth. And this was the only work God created on the second day.**" *Jubilees 2:4*

The Septuagint states: "**And God said, Let there be a firmament in the midst of the water, and let it be a division between water and water, and** it was so. And God made the firmament, and God divided between the water which was under the firmament and the water which was above the firmament. And God called the firmament Heaven, and God saw that it was good, and there was evening and there was morning, the second day." *Genesis 1:6-8*

On day three of the recreation, God gathered the waters from under the firmament into seas, thus after the dry land reappeared God recreated the grass, herbs, and trees bearing fruit, which without sunlight had disappeared. "And God said, let the water under the heaven be gathered together unto one place, and let the dry land appear: and it was so. And God called the dry land Earth; and the gathering together of the waters called he Seas; and God saw that it was good. And God said, let the earth bring forth grass, the herb yielding seed, and the fruit tree yielding fruit after his kind, whose seed is in in itself, after his kind: and God saw that it was good. And the evening and the morning were the third day." *Genesis 1:9-13*

The Book of Jubilees states: "And on the third day He commanded the waters to pass from off the face of the whole earth in to one place, and the dry land to appear. And the waters did so as He commanded them, and they retired from off the face of the earth into one place outside of this firmament, and the dry land appeared. And on that day He created for them all the seas according to their separate gathering-places, and all the rivers, and the gatherings of waters in the mountains and on all the earth, and all the lakes, and all the dew of the earth, and the seed which is sown, and all sprouting things, and fruit bearing trees, and trees of the wood, and the garden of Eden, in Eden and all plants after their kind. These four great works God created on the third day." *Jubilees 2:5-7*

The Septuagint states: "And God said, Let the water which is under the heaven be collected into one place, and let the dry land appear, and it was so. And the water which was under the heaven was collected into one place, and the dry land appeared. And God called the dry land Earth, and the gathering of the waters he called Seas, and God saw that it was good. And God said, Let the earth bring forth the herb of grass bearing seed according to its kind and according to its likeness, and the fruit-tree bearing fruit whose seed is in it, according to its kind on the earth, and it was so. And the earth brought forth the herb of grass bearing seed according to its kind and according to its likeness, and the fruit tree bearing fruit whose seed is in it, according to its kind on the earth, and God saw that it was good. And there was evening and there was morning, the third day." *Genesis 1:9-13*

On day four of the recreation, God dealt with the placement of the sun, moon, and the stars in heaven so as to once again be signs for seasons, and for days and nights, and years. When one considers the fact that there are literally billions of stars in countless constellations, our minds boggle at the fact that God knows the number and names of each one of them: "He telleth the number of the stars; he calleth them all by their names." *Psalms 147:4*

This truth is confirmed by a similar statement made by the prophet Isaiah who declares: "Lift up your eyes on high, and behold who hath created these (stars), that bringeth out their host by number: he calleth them all by names by the greatness of his might, for that he is strong in power; not one faileth." *Isaiah 40:26*

As far as we know the sun, moon and stars, which had been created in the beginning, had not been effected by Lucifer's rebellion. We are left to conclude that all the work of day four was in some way reconstructive, and not creative, thus it did not entail the creation of a new sun, moon, and stars. In other words, the work of day four may have been the realignment of the earth back on its original axis and orbit around the sun, in relation to our solar system. Because there is a difference of about ninety miles between true north, and magnetic north we know the Earth is still slightly off its original axis and slightly wobbles. That is why we today have a jet stream that vacillates and often causes severe weather patterns. To say it a third way, God commanded the sun, mood, and stars to be seen from the earth in a way as to renew their original purpose as signs for regulating the seasons, and to provide a greater light the a day, and a lesser light for the night. "And God said, let there be lights in the firmament of the heaven to divide the day from the night; and let them be for signs (owth-to mark, display, or signify), and for seasons, and for days and years: And let them be for lights in the firmament of the heaven to give light upon the earth: and it was so. And God made two great lights; the greater light to rule the day, and the lesser light to rule the night: he made the stars also.

And God set them in the firmament of the heaven to give light upon the earth, and to rule over the day and over the night, and to divide the light from the darkness; and God saw that it was good. And the evening and the morning were the fourth day." *Genesis 1:14-19*

The Book of Jubilees states: "And on the fourth day He created the sun and the moon and the stars, and set them in the firmament of the heaven, to give light upon all the earth, and to rule over the day and the night, and divide the light from the darkness. And God appointed the sun to be a great sign on the earth for days and for sabbaths anf for months and for feasts and for years and for sabbaths of year sand for jubilees and for all seasons of the year. And it divided the light from the darkness and for prosperity, that all things may prosper which shoot and grow on earth. These three kinds He made on the fourth day." *Jubilees 2:8-11*

The Septuagint states: "And God said Let there be lights in the firmament of the heaven to give light upon the earth, to divide between day and night, and let them be for signs and for seasons and for days and for years. And let them be for light in the firmament of the heaven, so as to shine upon the earth, and it was so. And God made the two great lights, for regulating the night, the stars also. And God placed them in the firmament of the heaven, so as to shine upon the earth, and to regulate day and night, and to divide between the light and the darkness. And God saw that it was good. And there was evening and there was morning, the fourth day." *Genesis 1:14-19*

On day five of the recreation, God recreated the birds of the air, and the fish of the seas and blessed them saying be fruitful and multiply, thus supplying mankind an abundant food supply for his nourishment. All animals have souls or feelings, personalities, emotions, desires, and appetites, but they are not made in the image of God, thus they are not eternal beings, but were made for the use of mankind. God's laws of reproduction dictates that each animal must reproduce after its own kind, thus, in nature different species normally cannot, or will not be cross bred. "And God said, let the waters bring forth abundantly the moving creature that hath life, and the fowl that may fly above the earth in the open firmament of heaven. And God created great whales, and every living creature that moveth, which the waters brought forth abundantly, after their kind, and every winged fowl after his kind: and God saw that it was good (towb-meaning precious or beautiful). And God blessed them, saying, be fruitful, and multiply, and fill the waters in the seas, and let fowl multiply in the earth. And the evening and the morning were the fifth day." *Genesis 1:20-23*

The Book of Jubilees states: "And on the fifth day He created great sea monsters in the depths of the waters, for these were the first things of flesh that were created by his hands, the fish and everything that moves in the waters, and everything that flies, the birds and all their kind. And the sun rose above them to prosper them, and above everything that was on the earth, everything that shoots out of the earth, and all fruit-bearing trees, and all flesh. These three kinds He created on the fifth day." *Jubilees 2:11-13*

The Septuagint states: "And God said, Let the waters bring forth reptiles having life, and winged creatures flying above the earth in the firmament of heaven, and it was so. And God made great whales, and every living reptile, which the waters brought forth according to their kinds, and evert creature that flies with wings according to its kind, and God saw that they were good. And God blessed them saying, Increase and multiply and fill the waters in the seas, and let the creatures that fly be multiplied on the earth. And there was evening and there was morning, the fifth day." *Genesis 1:20-23*

On the sixth day God recreated cattle and all manner of creeping things upon the earth after its own kind or species. This included all the different kinds of mammals, reptiles, insects, cattle, and every other kind of animal that lives on the surface of the earth. "And God said, let the earth bring forth the living creature after his kind, cattle, and creeping things, and beasts of the earth after his kind: and it was so. And god made the beast of the earth after their kind, and everything that creepeth upon the earth after his kind: and God saw that it was good." *Genesis 1:24-25*

On day six God also recreated man and women after his image and likeness to have dominion over the refurbished earth. The creation of mankind was the crowning act in God's plan to restore everything that had been destroyed by Lucifer's rebellion, and the Preadimite Flood. Many *Bible* teachers who believe and teach the Gap Theory, and the Preadamite Flood, are divided between two different opinions as to who the man and woman were who God created on the sixth day. Most *Bible* scholars believe that the man and woman created on the sixth day was Adam and Eve, but some teachers believe Adam and Eve were not created until the eighth day. What I am about to say now will certainly be controversial, and possibly confusing, thus, I will proceed very slowly. **"And God** (Elohom-Gods) **said, let us make man in our image** (tselem-form and fashon), **after our likeness: and let them have dominion** (radah-authority to subjugate) **over the fish of the sea, and over the foul of the air, and over the cattle, and over all the earth, and over every creeping thing that creepeth upon the earth. So God created man in his own image, in the image of God created he him; male and female created he them."** *Genesis 1:26-27*

The Book of Jubilees states: **"And on the sixth day He created all the animals of the earth, and all cattle, and everything that moves on the earth. And after all this He created man, a man and a woman created He them, and gave him dominion over all that is upon the earth, and in the seas, and over everything that flies, and over beasts and over cattle, and over everything that moves on the earth, and over the whole earth, and over all this He gave him dominion. And these four kinds He created on the sixth day. And there were together two and twenty kinds. And He finished all his work on the sixth day, all that is in the heavens and on the earth, and in the seas and in the abysses, and in the light and I the darkness, and in everything."** *Jubilees 2:13-17*

The Septuagint states: **"And God said, Let the earth bring forth the living creatures according to its kind, quadrupeds and reptiles and wild beasts of the earth according to their kind, and it was so. And God made the wild beasts of the earth according to their kind, and cattle according to their kind, and all the reptiles of the earth according to their kind, and God saw that they were good.**

And God said, Let us make man according to our image and likeness, and let them have dominion over the fish of the sea, and over the flying creatures of heaven, and over the cattle and all the earth, and over all the reptiles that creep on the earth. And God made man, according to the image of God he made him, male and female he made them. And God blessed them, saying, Increase and multiply, and fill the earth and subdue it, and have dominion over the fish of the sea and flying creatures of heaven, and

all the cattle and all the earth, and all the reptiles that creep on the earth.

And God said, Behold I have to you every seed-bearing herb sowing seed which is upon all the earth, and evert tree which has in itself the fruit of seed that is sown, to you it shall be for food, And to all the wild beasts of the earth, and to all the flying creatures of heaven, and to every reptile creeping on the earth, which has in itself the breath of life, even every green plant for food; and it was so. And God saw all the things that he had made, and, behold, they were very good. And there was evening and there was morning, the sixth day." *Genesis 1:24-31*

The dominion that Lucifer once exercised over the Preadamite Earth, and then abused, was on the sixth day of the recreated earth transferred and restored to the sixth day man and woman. Some theologians say the sixth day man and woman were created to be hunters and fishermen while Adam and Eve were called to be farmers. Again, are the man and woman created in the first chapter of *Genesis*, the same man and woman created in the second chapter of *Genesis*? The man and woman mentioned in the first chapter of *Genesis* was created on the sixth day, but were not named, and were never placed in a garden to till, and care for it. The man and woman created in the second chapter of *Genesis* were created on the eighth day and were named Adam and Eve. We are not told whether God created both the sixth day man and woman from the dust of the earth at the same time, or whether they were ever placed in a garden. We are also not told whether the sixth day man and woman were created at different times, and then placed in a garden, as was the case with Adam and Eve. It seems both the sixth day man and woman were created at the very same time, which again, was not the case with Adam and Eve. After God pronounced a blessing over both the sixth day man and women his first command to them was to immediately be fruitful and multiply in order to replenish, or repopulate the earth. "And God blesses them, and God said unto them, be fruitful and multiply, and replenish the earth, and subdue it: and have dominion over the fish of the sea, and over the fowl of the air, and over every living thing that moveth upon the earth." *Genesis 1:28*

Again, some *Bible* teachers believe the sixth day man and woman were not Adam and Eve, and were not living in the geographical region of the Garden of Eden. The sixth day man and woman were given complete freedom to eat from every fruit tree which was certainly not the case with Adam and Eve, and their descendants. "**And God said, Behold, I have given you every herb bearing seed, which is upon the face of all the earth, and every tree, in the which is the fruit of a tree yielding seed; to you it shall be meat. And to every beast of the earth, and to every fowl of the air, and to everything that creepeth upon the earth, wherein there is life, I have given every green herb for meat: and it was so. And God saw everything he had made, and behold, it was very good. And the evening and the morning were the sixth day.**" *Genesis 1:29-31*

On day seven God rested from all his recreation works, thus setting a president that all men, throughout time, should observe a Sabbath-day rest. Many scholars who teach the Gap Theory, and the Preadamite World, believe God went back to work on the eighth day by planting a garden east of Eden. According to this theory, God then created Adam (ha'adham), which means ruddy faced, or he who blushes red. Adam's job was to tend the Garden of Eden, and name all the animals which God had made in the six days of recreation. After all the animals were brought to him and named, Adam eventually realized that all the animals had mates, but he was alone, thus, only then did God create Eve. If the man and women created on the sixth day was not Adam and Eve, we then have the answer to the age-old question where did Cain get his wife?

Chapter 2

The Seed of the Woman

Now that I have presented the Preadamite World, and the Gap Theory, I would now like to present an even more controversial, and disputed theory, about Adam and Eve's sin in the Garden of Eden. God passed judgment on Lucifer, thus destroying the Preadamite World with a flood, and sadly, the exact same thing happened a second time after Adam and Eve's sin in the garden. I will attempt to present this theory in a simple, and understandable way, and again you should draw your own conclusions. After determining that all he had made during the six days of recreation was good, God rested on the seventh day. On the eighth day God chose to go back to work by creating Adam from the dust of the earth and placing him in a garden which contained both the tree of life, and the tree of the knowledge of good and evil. "**And the Lord God formed** (yatsar-to mold with the hand) **man of the dust of the ground, and breathed into his nostrils the breath of life; and man became a living soul. And the Lord God planted eastward in Eden; and there he put the man whom he had formed. And out of the ground made the Lord God to grow every tree that is pleasant to the sight, and good for food; the tree of life also in the midst of the garden, and the tree of the knowledge of good and evil.**" *Genesis 2:7-9*

God made Adam to be a gardener, whose first job was to prune and care for the Garden of Eden. God then gave Adam only one restriction, that being not to eat of the tree of the knowledge of good and evil, or death would soon follow that same day. Adam could eat from all the other trees, but that one tree in the middle of the garden, fascinated him the most. The tree probably looked to Adam to be a great food source, but God had warned that it was quite deadly. "**And the Lord God took the man, and put him into the Garden of Eden to dress it and to keep it. And the Lord God commanded the man, saying, of every tree of the garden thou mayest freely eat. But of the tree of the knowledge of good and evil, thou shalt not eat of it: for in the day that thou eatest thereof thou shall surely die.**" Genesis *2:15-17*

After Adam came to the recognition that, unlike all the animals God had just made, he was without a mate to help him tend the garden, and repopulate the earth. God determined that it was not good for Adam to be alone thus God made for him a life partner capable of helping him accomplish all that God would call him to do. This woman would not be created from the red clay of the ground as was the case with Adam, but from the flesh and ribs of Adam's side, thus she became flesh of Adam's flesh, and bone of Adam's bones." **And the Lord God caused a deep sleep to fall upon Adam, and he slept: and he took one of his ribs, and closed up the flesh instead thereof. And the rib, which the Lord God had taken from man, made he a woman, and brought her unto the man. And Adam said, this is now bone of my bones, and flesh of my flesh: she shall be called woman, because she was taken out of man."** Genesis *2:21-23*

Adam and Eve were now one flesh and together they walked naked throughout the garden and were not ashamed. Neither of them had a since of shame or awareness of sin for they had not yet broke the one negative commandment God had given them. Daily they walked and tended the garden and in the cool of the evening they both communed and talked with God. We are not told what God may have said to Adam and Eve, or whether he further warned them about the serpent's connection with the tree of the knowledge of good and evil. **"Now the serpent was more subtle than any beast of the field which the Lord God had made. And he said unto the woman, Yea, hath God said, ye shall not eat of every tree of the garden? And the woman said unto the serpent, we may eat of the fruit of the trees of the garden: But of the fruit of the tree which is in the midst of the garden, God hath said, ye shall not eat of it, neither shall ye touch** (naga-have sex) **it, lest ye die."** *Genesis* 3: 1-3

Here Lucifer, through the form of a serpent, is clearly trying to deceive and seduce Eve into disobeying Gods word. Is this the way Lucifer deceived and defiled the people of the Preadamite World? In essence what Lucifer was tempting Eve with was becoming independent in her thoughts and deeds from God, the very sin that had gotten him in trouble with God. Lucifer continued the deception of Eve by suggesting that God was a liar when he warned them both that death would soon follow if they ate from the forbidden fruit. Lucifer then goes further in his deception by offering Eve wisdom, eternal life, and equality with God. **"And the serpent said unto the woman, ye shall not surly die: For God doth know that in the** day ye eat thereof, then your eyes shall be opened, and ye shall be as gods, knowing good and evil. And when the Woman saw that the tree was good for food, and that it was pleasant to the eyes, and a tree to be desired to make one wise, she took of the fruit thereof, and did eat, and gave also unto her husband with her; and he did eat" Genesis 3:4-6

The Apostle Paul clearly taught the Corinthian Church that Eve was completely seduced by the serpent, or Satan, when he wrote his second letter to the Corinthians, telling them they should be chased virgins unto the Lord. "For I am jealous over you with godly jealously: for I have espoused you to one husband that I may present you as a chased virgin to Christ. But I fear, lest by any means, as the serpent beguiled (exapatao-completely seduced) Eve through his subtility, so your minds should be corrupted from the simplicity that is in Christ." II Corinthians 11:2-3

It is important to insert here a very controversial doctrine that is taught by a number of Hebrew scholars concerning Eve's seduction. They teach that both Adam and Eve had sex with Satan, by way of the serpent. They further teach that from this sexual union Eve became pregnant and gave birth to Cain, thus while Adam was the father of Able, Satan was the true father of Cain. As proof of this they point to the fact that Cain is not listed in Adam's gerontology. According to this doctrine the descendants of Cain from that time forward were known as Kenites, which are mentioned several times throughout the *Old Testament*, and were literally the Seed of Satan. Again, according to this theory, the scribes and Pharisees who conspired to kill Jesus were descended from the Kenites. "Ye are of your father the devil, and the lusts of your father ye will do. He was a murderer from the beginning, and abode not in the truth, because there is no truth in him. When he speaketh a lie, he speaketh of his own: for he is a liar, and the father of it." *John* 8:44

The main problem with this doctrine is if the Kenites were the descendants of Cain, and are mentioned throughout the *Old Testament*, how did they survive Noah's Flood? There were only eight people saved in the Ark, thus the descendants of Cain must have perished in the flood. "And God spake unto Noah, saying, go forth of the Ark, thou, and thy wife, and thy sons, and thy sons' wives with thee." Genesis 8:15-16

After eating of the forbidden fruit Adam and Eve's eyes were opened to the reality of sin and gained a since of shame which caused them to immediately hide from God. While hiding, Adam and Eve try to hide their shame by sewing fig leaves together in order to hide their private parts with aprons. Why did Adam and Eve immediately make aprons in order to hide their private parts? Could sex have played a part in this deception, and seduction? **"And the eyes of them both were opened, and they knew that they were naked; and they sewed fig leaves together, and made themselves aprons. And they heard the voice of the Lord God walking in the garden in the cool of the day: and Adam and his wife hid themselves from the presence of the Lord God amongst the trees of the garden. And the Lord God called unto Adam, and said unto him, where art thou? And he said, I heard thy voice in the garden, and I was afraid, because I was naked; and I hid myself."** Genesis *3:7-10*

God replied to Adam's confession, by asking him two questions. Who told you that you were naked? Have you eaten of the tree I commanded you not to eat from? Instead of blaming himself for disobeying God's command, Adam blames the whole thing on Eve, who, in turn, blames everything on the serpent. **"And the man said, the woman whom thou gavest to be with me, she gave me of the tree, and I did eat. And the Lord God said unto the woman, what is this that thou hast done? And the woman said, the serpent beguiled me, and I did eat."** Geneses *3:12-13*

God then confronts the serpent but unlike Adam and Eve, he does not ask him to give an account of his actions because what he did was not unexpected. Instead God immediately pronounces a curse upon the serpent, which confines it to forever crawl on its belly in the dust of the earth. This curse indicates that whatever form the serpent took when seducing Eve, it previously did not crawl on its belly, but instead stood upright, and walked on its feet. **"And the Lord God said unto the serpent, because thou hast done this, thou art cursed above all the cattle, and above every beast of the field; upon thy belly shalt thou go, and dust shalt thou eat all the days of thy life."** Genesis *3:14*

At this point God directs his words beyond the physical serpent to Lucifer, the spiritual outlaw energizing, anointing, and directing the serpent. As stated in the previous chapter, God, in pronouncing this judgement on Lucifer, was careful not to say too much. God would pass judgement on Lucifer again as he had done in the Preadamite World, but would say only that he and his followers would one day be defeated. **"And I will enmity between thee and the woman, and between thy seed and her seed; it shall bruise thy head, and thou shall bruise his heel."** Genesis *3:15*

Without giving away any details, God has just told Lucifer that a direct descendent of Eve would one day deal him a deadly blow, and take back from him the spiritual dominion over the earth he had just stolen from Adam. I choose to call this mystery an open conspiracy, for God in his foreknowledge published and displayed this truth for all to see in the stars. Before Moses wrote down the Pentateuch, the first five books of the *Old Testament* in about 1460 BC, there was no written record of man's fall or of the gospel of redemption through the Seed of the Woman. Modern-day occultists often refer to these star signs as the Zodiac, but the ancient Hebrews always called them the Mazzaroth, which means the star signs. According to ancient Hebrew traditions, Ham taught his son Cush, who in turn taught his son Nimrod the true signs and meanings of the Mazzaroth but he turned them into idols and changed their name to the Mazzalah. It was Nimrod who first turned the Mazzaroth into the zodiac when he turned the twelve signs into gods in their own right, and displayed them at the base of the Tower of Babble. Said another way, in their rebellion to God the Babylonians, under Nimrod's leadership, perverted the true study of the Mazzaroth, which was called astronomy, into worshiping the Mazzalah, which is now called astrology, the study of the Horoscope. The seven stars of the Pleiases, and the three stars of Orions' Belt are mentioned in the *Bible*. For a better understanding of God's true Mazzaroth, I suggest reading Marilyn Hickiey's book *Signs in the Heavens*. As we shall see in a following chapter, Abram's father Terah, during the days of Nimrod, worshiped theses same twelve signs of the zodiac in his house. Abram was told by God to leave his father's house in Ur of the Chaldeans, and resettle in the Land of Canaan. According to ancient Jewish tradition, after God told him to leave Ur, Abram could no longer tolerate the worship of these twelve gods by his father, thus he took his family and moved out of his father's house to Haren, about six hundred miles north of Ur. When Abram was seventy five years old he took his family and household servants and then moved from Haran toward the Land of Canaan. God was not opposed to the study and understanding of his Mazzaroth, but to worship the Mazzalah or Zodiac was idolatry. God said to Job: **"Canst thou bind the sweet influences of Pleiades, or loose the bands of Orion? Canst thou bring forth Mazza-**

roth in his season? Or canst thou guide Arcturus with his sons? Knowest thou the ordinances of heaven? Canst thou set the dominion thereof in the earth?" Job 38:31

"And he (King Josiah) put down the idolatrous priests, whom the kings of Juda had ordained to burn incense in the high places in the cities of Judah, and in the places round about Jerusalem; them also that burned incense unto Baal, to the sun, and to the moon, and to the planets (Mazzalah), and to all the host of heaven." II Kings 23:5

"Seek him that maketh the seven stars of Orion, and turneth the shadow of death into the morning, and maketh the day dark with night." Amos 5:8

"Which maketh Arcturus, Orion, and Pleiades, and the chambers of the south." Job 9:9

When Nimrod changed the Mazzaroth to the Mazzalath he divided the twelve constellations into smaller constellations called decans, thus he in essence created twelve gods who supposedly can exercise some type of influence over every person on earth. Author Ken Johnson, in his book *Ancient Paganism* states: "The idea of astrology was to find out what could happen to a particular person on a specific day. If Mars or Venus was in the right position based on where they were when that person was born, then their finances or love life might improve if they acted today. Or, perhaps, today may not be the best time for that person to start a fight or business."

The religion started by Nimrod and his wife Semiramis is the foundation of all false pagan religions in the earth today, and the study of the Nimrod's Zodiac is the foundation of most new-age religions plaguing America today. The Constellations have absolutely no effect or control over a person's life, but unfortunately Satan does. "The heavens declare the glory of God; and the firmament sheweth his handiwork. Day unto day uttereth speech, and night unto night sheweth knowledge. There is no speech nor language, where their voice is not heard. Their line is gone out through all the earth, and their words to the end of the world. In them hath he set a tabernacle for the sun." *Psalms 19:1-4*

"Remember the former things of old: for I am God, and there is none else; I am God, and there is none like me. Declaring the end from the beginning, and from ancient times the things that are not yet done, saying, my counsel shall stand, and I will do all my pleasure." Isaiah 46:9-10

The mystery that has been hidden from the foundation of the newly recreated earth is that a virgin would conceive and bring forth a second Adam. This last Adam would one day appear, stripping Lucifer of his dominion over the earth, and restoring the spiritual life and dominion that the first Adam had lost. "For since by man came death, by man came also the resurrection of the dead. For as in Adam all die, even so in Christ shall all be made alive." I Corinthians 15:21-22

Lucifer never dreamed that the godhead would have conspired together to send the Son of God to earth in the physical form of a second or last Adam. The Apostil Paul went on to reveal this mystery to the Corinthian Church saying: "And so it is written, the first man Adam was made a living soul; the last Adam was made a quickening (life giving) spirit." I Corinthians 15:45

The Apostle Paul further revealed details of this mystery to the Roman Church saying: "Wherefore, as by one man sin entered into the world, and death by sin; and so death passed upon all men, for that all have sinned. For until the law sin was in the world: but sin is not inputed when there is no law. Nevertheless death reigned from Adam to Moses, even over them that had not sinned after the similitude of Adam's transgression." Romans 5:12-14

Would Lucifer have ever dreamed that God himself would have impregnated a virgin and then left heaven to be born a physical man on this earth? "Therefore the Lord himself shall give you a sign. Behold, a virgin shall conceive and bear a son, and shall call his name Immanuel." Isaiah 7:14

As stated earlier, this ancient mystery, or open conspiracy, has been foretold in the stars, which God originally made to be sighs for all men to see. Several Bible scholars believe the ancient sighs of the Zodiac originally had far different meanings than are attributed to it today by modern-day astrologists, and witches. Author E. Raymond Capt, in his book The Glory of the Stars states: "Virgo is pictured as a woman with a branch in her right hand and some ears of corn in her left hand. The name of this sign in Hebrew is Betulah, which means a virgin: in Greek, Parthenos, the maid of virgin pureness: in Arabic, Adarah, the pure virgin. All the traditions, names and mythologies, connected with this sign, recognize and emphasized the virginity of the woman. But, the greater wonder is that motherhood attends the virginity. About one hundred years before Christ an alter was found in Gall (France) with this inscription: 'To the virgin who is to bring forth.' This woman in the sign is the holder and bringer of an illustrious seed."

Another *Bible* schollar, E.W. Bullinger, in his book *The Witness of the Stars* states: "The Greeks, ignorant of the Divine origin and teaching of the sign, represented Virgo as Ceres, with ears of corn in her hand. In the Zodiac in the Temple of Denderah, in Egypt, about 2000 BC (now in Paris), she is likewise represented with a branch in her hand, but ignorantly explained by a false religion to represent Isis! Her name is called Aspolia, which means ears of corn, or the seed, which shows that through the woman is seen, it is her seed who is the great subject of the prophecy." Bullinger further states: "The first constellation in Virgo explains that this coming branch will be a child, and that he should be the desire of all nations."

At this point we need to investigate further into just what was the nature of Adam and Eve's transgression. After their sin in the garden, the punishment and curses they both receive reflects some light upon their individual sin. Both had sinned, but which one did Gold hold to be most responsible for being seduced by the serpent: "**And the Lord God said unto the women. What is this that thou hast done? And the woman said, the serpent beguiled (nasha-seduced) me, and I did eat.**" *Genesis 3:13*

God then places a curse on Eve that reflects the nature of her sin which was conception. "**Unto the women he said, I will greatly multiply thy sorrow and thy conception; in sorrow thou shalt bring forth children; and thy desire shall be to thy husband, and he shall rule over thee.**" *Genesis 3:16*

Was Eve being cursed because she had given the forbidden fruit to her husband, or could something even more sinister have taken place? Eve's curse had four major points to it, that being conception, child birth, sexual desire, and male domination. Could Eve's seduction have involved more than just the eating of a forbidden fruit, or could intercourse somehow have taken place? Could Eve's sexual desire not have been to her husband, but turned rather toward the serpent instead? The *Bible* simply does not come out and tell us this for a fact, thus leaving us to try and read between the lines. Could sexual intercourse be what Paul warned of when speaking to the Corinthians: **"For I am jealous over you with godly jealousy: for I have espoused you to one husband that I may present you as a chaste virgin to Christ. But I fear, lest by any means, as the serpent beguiled Eve through his subtlety, so your minds should be corrupted from the simplicity that is in Christ."** *II Corinthians 11: 2-4*

Not that the *Bible* said she did, but the fact that Eve could have gotten pregnant by such a union be why God pronounced the curse of painful child birth upon the daughters of Eve? Could Eve's possible unfaithfulness to Adam, be why God punished her by stating she should forever be ruled over by her husband? Was this what Paul was speaking of when he said: **"For this cause ought the women to have power** (exoosseah- meaning mastery-freedom-control or jurisdiction) **on her head because of the angels** (fallen angels)." *I Corinthians 11:10*

God's major condemnation of Adam came from the fact that he had given more credence to Eve's words than to God's commandments. Adam was standing next to Eve during the temptation by the serpent and had failed to say even a word. Eve was the one that spoke to the serpent and argued with him about what God had commanded them about eating the fruit of the trees of the garden. **"And the woman said unto the serpent, we may eat of the fruit of the trees of the garden. But of the fruit of the tree which is in the midst of the garden, God hath said, ye shall not eat of it, neither shall ye touch it, lest ye die. And the serpent said unto the woman, ye shall not surely die."**

Just by reading between the lines, it seems that Adam had also not been faithful to work and tend the Garden because increased weeds, and reduced fertility was his punishment: **"And unto Adam he said, because thou has harkened unto the voice of thy wife, and hast eaten of the tree, of which I commanded thee, saying, thou shalt not eat of it: cursed is the ground for thy sake; in sorrow shalt thou eat of it all the days of thy life. Thorns also and thistles shall it bring forth to thee; and thou shall eat the herb of the field. In the sweat of thy face shalt thou eat bread, till thou return** unto the ground; for out of it was thou taken: for dust thou art, and unto dust shalt thou return." *Genesis 3:17-19*

Adam had not been seduced and deceived in the same way Eve had been, thus, we are left to conclude that he freely chose to eat of the forbidden fruit, possibly, not wanting to be separated from her in judgement. Although the *Bible* does not tell us all the details of what took place in the Garden of Eden, it is safe to say that Eve had not as yet been impregnated by Adam, which God had commanded. **"And Adam was not deceived, but the woman being deceived was in the transgression. Notwithstanding she shall be saved in childbearing, if they continue in faith and charity and holiness with sobriety."** *I Timothy 2:14-15*

Adam and eve had at first attempted to cover their nakedness by sewing together fig leaves, but now God makes for them coats of skin to clothe their nakedness. Whatever the true nature of their individual sins may have been, Adam and Eve's fellowship with God was now broken and they were immediately ushered out of the garden, lest they eat of the tree of life and live forever in a cursed state: **"Unto Adam also and to his wife did the Lord God make coats of skins, and clothed them. And the Lord God said, Behold, the man is become as one of us, to know good and evil: and now, lest he put forth his hand, and take also of the tree of life, and eat, and live forever."** *Genesis 3:21-22*

After being driven out of the garden, Adam struggled to feed himself and Eve. Any thoughts of returning to the garden however was out of the question for God had placed angels, or Cherubim outside the entrances to the garden. A mysterious flaming sward that turned in every direction, was placed in the middle of the garden where the Tree of Life was located, to guard it. Before their sin, Adam and Eve could freely eat of this tree and live forever, but now, they would be subject to death: **"Therefore the Lord God sent him forth from the garden of Eden, to till the ground from whence he was taken. So he drove out the man; and he placed at the east of the garden of Eden Cherubims, and a flaming sward which turned every way, to keep the way of the tree of life."** *Genesis 3:23-24*

At this point about the only thing Lucifer knew for sure about God's secret plan to eventually crush his head was that it would come about through the seed, or the descendants of Eve. After Eve bore Cain and Abel, it is quite likely that Lucifer watched every move the two brothers made, hoping one day to kill them both. Cain like Adam, was a gardener and produced fruit and vegetables from the ground. Abel, on the other hand was a keeper of sheep, thus, when both brothers brought offerings to God, only Abel's fat offering was acceptable to God. This brought strife between the two brothers, which Lucifer saw as an opportunity to kill one, if not both of them: **"And Cain talked with Abel his brother: and it came to pass, when they were in the field, that Cain rose against Abel his brother, and slew him "** *Genesis 4:8*

At this point those who believe in the gap-theory point out that there had to have been two different groups of people on the earth for Cain to be concerned that if he becoming a fugitive and vagabond on the earth, strangers would try to capture, and kill him. Secondly, if Cain could have found a wife in the Land of Nod, there must have been a totally different group of people living in the Land of Nod. **"Behold, thou hast driven me out this day from the face of the earth; and from thy face shall I be hid; and I shall be a fugitive and a vagabond in the earth; and it shall come to pass, that every one that findeth me shall slay me,"** *Genesis 4:14*

With Abel dead, and Cain now cursed and driven far away from his family, east of Eden into the land of Nod, Eve again produced another son named Seth. It would be through Seth, and his seed that God would one day produce the second, or last Adam that would ultimately crush Lucifer's head. Lucifer could only suspect this to be true but he had no proof to go on for God remained silent on the matter: **"And Adam knew his wife again; and she bare a son, and called his name Seth. For God, said she, hath appointed me another seed instead of Abel, whom Cain slew. And to Seth, to him also there was born a son; and he called his name Enos: then began men to call upon the name of the Lord."** *Genesis 4:25-26*

Unfortunately the *Bible* does not give us an abundance of historical information about either Cain or Seth, thus, we are left to depend on the traditions taught by various Jewish historians such as Josephus. According to these traditions Cain, after moving east to the Land of Nod, founded a city named Enoch after his firstborn son Enoch. It is important to remember this is not the same seventh generation from Adam Enoch who walked with God. In time the decedents of Seth founded cities along the four rivers, the Pison, Gihon, Hiddekel, and Euphrates which flowed out of the Garden of Eden. The descendants of Seth remained faithful to God for seven generations until they were badly influenced by the descendants of Cain.

Josephus states: "Now this posterity of Seth continued to esteem God as Lord of the universe, and to have an entire regard to virtue, for seven generations; but in the process of time they were perverted, and forsook the practices of their forefathers; and did neither pay those honors to God which were appointed them, towards men, nor had they any concern to do justice towards men. But for what degree of zeal they had formerly shown for virtue, they now showed by their actions a double degree of wickedness, whereby they made God to be their enemy."

At this point some of the Sethites began to intermarry with the Cainites and adopted their evil ways, thus polluting the bloodline of the promised seed through Seth. Josephus states: "Even while Adam was alive, it came to pass that the posterity of Cain became exceeding wicked, every one successively dying, one after another, more wicked than the former. They were intolerable in war, and vehement in robberies; and if anyone were slow to murder people, yet was he bold in his profligate behavior, in acting unjustly, and doing injuries for gain."

Noah, being a preacher of righteousness preached to this generation, trying to persuade them to give up their violent and perverted ways and turn back to God, but they turned to idolatry instead. The gospel of the redeemer was visible for them all to see in the heavens, but their foolish hearts were darkened so that they were no longer able to discern the truth, thus the mystery of the coming seed of the woman was lost to them. "For that which is known about God is evident to them and made plain in their inner consciousness, because God Himself has shown it to them. For ever since the creation of the world His invisible nature and attributes, that is, His eternal power and divinity, have been made intelligible and clearly discernable in and through the things that have been made, His handiwork. So men are without excuse altogether without any defense or justification.

Because when they knew and recognized Him as God, they did not honor and glorify Him as God or give Him thanks. But instead they became futile and godless in their thinking with vain imaginings, foolish reasoning, and stupid speculations and their senseless minds were darkened.

Claiming to be wise, they became fools professing to be smart, they made simpletons of themselves. And by them the glory and majesty and excellence of the immortal God were exchanged for and represented by images, resembling mortal man and birds and beasts and reptiles.

Therefore God gave them up in the lusts of their own hearts to sexual impurity, to the dishonoring of their bodies among themselves abandoning them to the degrading power of sin. Because they exchanged the truth of God for a lie and worshiped and served the creature rather than the Creator, Who is blessed forever!" *Romans 1:19-25* AMP

Chapter 3

The Counterfeit Seed

After being evicted from the Garden of Eden, Adam and Eve's children proceeded to repopulate the earth as God had commanded them. All the time Lucifer was standing off in the shadows, biding his time, and watching the descendants of Adam and Eve. One of those seeds would one day crush his head, but which one, for now there were beginning to be so many? When Lucifer rebelled against God, a third of the Angels of heaven rebelled also and became spiritual outlaws with him. As Lucifer's allies, we can be sure that these fallen angels were watching the descendants of Adam and Eve also. This observation continued until one day Lucifer and his band of rebels saw a new opportunity to thwart God's judgement upon them. If Lucifer could not kill off all the descendants of Eve, the next best thing to do would be to pollute them so as to destroy their seed line, thus eliminating the promised seed. The Sons of God, or angels, saw the daughters of man and took wives of them both before and after Noah's Flood. As we shall see in the next chapter of this book, this act of rebellion so corrupted the recreated world system that Noah's Flood would soon be needed **"And it came to pass, when men began to multiply on the face of the earth, and daughters were born unto them, That the Sons of God** (Bene HaElohim-Sons of God) **saw the daughters of men** (Benoth Adom-Daughters of Adam) **that they were fair; and they took wives of all which they chose."** *Genesis 6:1-2*

This rebellion so hurt God and enraged him to the point that he reduced man's lifespan from several hundred, to only one hundred and twenty years. The reason for God's anger is clearly because he had just spent six days recreating the earth, and recreating man to repopulate it. Now we have a hybrid man, half angel and half man, which throughout the *Old Testament* is referred to by various names such as the Avims, Gibborim, Anakim, Zuzim, Zamzummim, Ahiman, Sheshai, Talmai, Emim, Horim, and Rephaim. Throughout the Bible the name Nephilim is usually used for the fallen angels, and their offspring the giants are usually called the Rephaim. "**There were giants in the earth in those days; and also after that** (after Noah's Flood), **when the sons of God came in unto the daughters of men, and they bare children to them, the same became mighty men** (Gibborim) **which were of old, men of renown.**" *Genesis 6:4*

The *Septuagint* states: "**And it came to pass when men began to be numerous upon the earth, daughters were born to them, that the sons of God having seen the daughters of men that they were beautiful, took to themselves wives of all whom they chose. And the Lord God said, My Spirit shall certinly not remain among these men for ever, because they are flesh, but their days shall be an hundred and twenty years. Now the giants were upon the earth in those days; and after that when the sons of God were wont to go in to the daughters of men, they bore children to them, those were the giants of old, the men of renound.**" *Genesis 6:2-5*

The *Book of Jasher* states: "**But in the latter days of Methuselah, the sons of men turned from the Lord; they corrupted the earth, they robbed and plundered each other, and they rebelled against God; they went contrary to God. They corrupted their ways, and would not listen to the voice of Methuselia, but rebelled against him.**" *Jasher 4:4*

The *Book of Jubilees* states: "**And after this they sinned against the beasts and birds, and all that moveth and walketh on the earth: and every imagination and desire of men imagined vanity and evil continually.**" *Jubilees 7:24*

Moses informs us that the corrupting of mankind, as well as the animal kingdom resulted in the giants being born, and later dwelling in the Promised Land. Moses stated: "**The Emims dwelt therein in times past, a people great, and many, and tall, as the Anakims. Which also were accounted giants, as the Anakims; but the Moabites call them Emims. The Horims also dwelt in Seir beforetime; but the children of Esau succeeded them, when they destroyed them from before them and dwelt in their stead.**" *Deuteronomy 2:10-12*

"**That also was accounted a land of giants: giants dwelt therein in old time; and the Ammonites call them Zamzummims.**" *Deuteronomy 2:20*

There had been only eight generations between Adam and Noah, but with Lucifer and his angel's interference, mankind was again so polluted and sinful that their every thought was only to do evil. God was so hurt by this rebellion, that he said he was sorry he had ever made man, and regretted that he would again have to judge and destroy him. **"And God saw that the wickedness of man was great in the earth, and that every imagination of the thoughts of his heart was only evil continually. And it repented the Lord that he had made man on the earth, and it grieved him at his heart. And the Lord said, I will destroy man whom I have created from the face of the earth; both man, and beast, and the creeping thing, and the fowls of the air; for it repenteth me that I have made them."** *Genesis 6: 5-7*

The Septuagint states: **"And the Lord God, having seen that the wicked actions of men were multiplied upon the earth, and that everyone in his heart was intently brooding over evil continually, then God laid it to heart that he had made man upon the earth, and he pondered it deeply. And God said, I will blot out man whom I have made from the face of the earth, even man with cattle, and reptiles with flying creatures of the sky, for I am grieved that I have made them."** *Genesis 6:6-8*

Jesus told us that as it was in the day of Noah, so will it be in the last days just before his second coming. If we are indeed living in the last days, we can deduct that what we see happening now must have been happening in Noah's Day. If wastewater injection wells are causing earthquakes in our day, just imagine how many earthquakes must have happened when the flood waters of Noah's Flood began migrating back underground after the flood? If atheistic scientists are secretly genetically engineering, and cloning chimeras by doing gene splicing on different species of plants and animals, then what was happening in Noah's day? If today we are combining human body parts with compatible mechanical devices to create transhumans, then what were the days of Noah like? In Noah's day I believe there really were creatures that were half fish and half human called Mermaids, and half horse, and half human creatures called Centaurs. I further believe there were half goat and half human creatures called Satyrs, and half human and half bull creatures called Minotaurs. Jesus said: **"But as in the days of Noah were, so shall also the coming of the Son of man be, For as in the days that were before the flood they were eating and drinking, marrying and giving in marriage, until the day that Noah entered into the ark, And knew not until the flood came, and took them all away, so** shall also the coming of the Son of man be." *Mathew 24:37-39*

With the birth of the giants, mankind was faced with the pollution of its bloodline, which God had to deal with if the pure seed of the woman was to ever be born. God looked down upon the earth to see whose bloodline had not yet been polluted by the Nephilim. The word Nephilim means fallen one, which points to the fallen angels who fathered them. The giants, and their escapades represents the grain of truth within Egyptian, Greek, and Roman mythology concerning the demigods and the heroes of Olympus. It explains the mythology of Gaia the mother of the Titans, the offspring of the gods. It explains the true story about Nimrod, who was a real giant, and his wife Semiramis, who was the origin of almost all pagan gods and goddess worship. In Greek and Roman mythology there were many of these heroes such as Aeneas the son of Venus, Minos the son of Zeus, Bellerophon the son of Poseidon, Romulus and Remus the two sons of Mars, and of course Hercules the son of Jupiter. God was faced with the problem of once again destroying the earth, without destroying the bloodline of Adam and Eve. God found the answer to this problem when he looked down and found a family who were still perfect in their genealogy, and capable of producing the Seed of the Woman. **"And God saw that the wickedness of man was great in the earth, and that every imagination of the thoughts of his heart was only evil continually. And it repented the Lord that he had made man on the earth, and it grieved him at his heart. And the Lord said, I will destroy man whom I have created from the face of the earth; both man, and beast, and the creeping thing, and the fouls of the air; for it repenteth me that I have made them. But Noah found grace in the eyes of the Lord. These are the generations of Noah: Noah was a just man and perfect (Tamiym-unblemished) in his generations, and Noah walked with God."** *Genesis 6: 5-9*

Noah and his family was saved, not just because he was just, and walked with God. Noah was not saved just because he was a preacher of righteousness, but because he was perfect, or untainted in his generations or genealogy. His family's bloodline had not yet been polluted by the giants. **"And the Lord said unto Noah, come thou and all thy house into the ark, for thee have I seen righteous before me in this generation."** *Genesis 7:1*

"And Noah did according unto all that the Lord commanded him. And Noah was six hundred years old when the flood of waters was upon the

earth. And Noah went in, and his sons, and his wife, and his son's wives with him, into the ark, because of the waters of the flood." *Genesis 7:5-7*

"And it came to pass in the six hundredth and first year, in the first month, the first day of the month, the waters were dried up from off the earth: and Noah removed the covering of the Ark, and looked, and behold, the face of the ground was dry." *Genesis 8:13*

"And God spake unto Noah, saying, go forth of the Ark, thou and thy wife, and thy sons, and thy son's wives with thee." *Genesis 8:15-16*

"And God blessed Noah and his sons, and said unto them, be fruitful, and multiply, and replenish the earth" *Genesis 9:1*

"And you, be ye fruitful, and multiply; bring forth abundantly in the earth, and multiply therein. And God spake unto Noah, and to his sons with him, saying, And I, behold, I establish my covenant with you, and with your seed after you." *Genesis 9:7-9*

"And Noah began to be an husbandman, and he planted a vineyard. And he drank of the wine, and was drunken; and he was uncovered within his tent. And Ham, the father of Canaan, saw the nakedness of his father, and told his two brethren without." *Genesis 9:20-22*

Nobody wants to see their parents naked, and it is not a sin to do so, but this is not what has happened here. The sad truth is that both Noah and his wife were passed out naked when Ham, found them both in the tent. Ham took sexual advantage of his inebriated mother and when Noah awoke he was broken hearted and ashamed because of this incident. To accidentally see a parent naked is not a sin, but to uncover your mother for the purpose of having sex with her is unconceivable to any normal person. "The nakedness of thy father, or the nakedness of thy mother, shalt thou not uncover: she is thy mother; thou shalt not uncover her nakedness. The nakedness of thy father's wife shall thou not uncover: it is thy father's nakedness." *Leviticus 18:7-8*

The *Moffat Bible* translation makes what is said here very plain. Moffat states: "You shall not have intercourse with any wife of your father." *Leviticus 18-8*

"And the man that lieth with his father's wife hath uncovered his father's nakedness: both of them shall surely be put to death; their blood shall be upon them" *Leviticus 20:11*

This bizarre act of incest produced Canaan, who a few years later would be cursed by his grandfather Noah. It seems somewhat strange that Noah would curse Canaan for what his father Ham had done unless Canaan had already been born, and it was Canaan who committed incest. **"And Noah awoke from his wine, and knew what his younger son had done to him. And he said, Cursed be Canaan; a servant of servants shall he be unto his brethren. And he said, blessed be the Lord God of Shem; and Canaan shall be his servant. God shall enlarge Japheth, and he shall dwell in the tents of Shem; and Canaan shell be his servant. And Noah lived after the flood three hundred and fifty years. And all the days of Noah were nine hundred and fifty years: and he died."** *Genesis 9:24-29*

Just as Lucifer, and his fallen angels had earlier closely watched the seed of Adam and Eve, with Noah now dead they closely watched his descendants, to discover who the promised seed might be. It was at this point that the fallen angels again repeated the same sin that had brought on the judgement of Noah's Flood. The sin of Ham, and the resulting curse on his descendants seems to have provided a perfect opportunity for Lucifer to eliminate Ham's family from producing the Promised seed. The second invasion from heaven by the fallen angels seems to have been aimed mostly at Ham's four sons Cush, Mizraim, Phut, and Canaan. Ham and his four sons unfortunately taught the post-food people of the earth the abominable sins and idolatry that had existed before the flood. Jesus predicted that there would be a third eruption of the fallen angels on earth just before his second coming. **"For as in the days that were before the flood they** (the fallen angels) **were eating and drinking, marrying and giving in marriage, until the day that Noah entered into the ark."** *Matthew 24:38*

After the flood, Ham, and his two sons Phut and Mizraim moved and settled along the Nile River in what would later become known as Egypt. Canaan moved a couple of hundred miles from Egypt, to what would later become known as the Land of Canaan, today known as Palestine. Cush and Nimrod moved to the Land of Shinar, today known as Iraq, thus sin began to spread everywhere by these four sons. Author Ken Johnson, in his book *Ancient Paganism* states: **"Both the ancient rabbis and church fathers** taught that Egypt was the first to bring back the magic system of the pre-flood world. This started to spread into various countries through the sons of Ham, according to the Jewish history book of jubilees. This occurred after Canaan started settling the coast of Canaan/Israel." The fallen angels had first polluted the blood line of all those living before the flood, now all the people living after the flood were faced with the same problem. "There were giants in the earth in those days (before the flood); and also after that (after the flood), when the sons of God came in unto the daughters of men, and they bare children to them, the same became mighty men which were of old, men of renown." *Genesis 6:4*

Ham's son Cush begat six sons, Seba, Havilah, Sabtah, Raamah, Sabtechah, and Nimrod. Cush had sex with one of his daughters Semimaris, who gave birth to Nimrod. Ham's son Mizrain begat Ludim, Anamim, Lehabim, Naphtuhim, Pathrusim, and Casluhim. The children of Ham's son Phut are not listed in scripture. The exact number of the sons produced by Canaan is unknown, but some are mentioned throughout the *Old Testament* as living in the geographical area of Canaan, or Palestine, and many of them were giants. "And Canaan begat Sidon his first born, and Heth, and the Jebusite, and the Amorite, and the Girgasite, and the Hivite, and the Arkite, and the Sinite, and the Arvadite, and the Zemarite, and the Hamathite: and afterward were the families of the Canaanites spread abroad. And the border of the Canaanites was from Sidon, as thou comest to Gerar, unto Gaza; as thou goest, unto Sodom, and Gomorah, and Admah, and Zeboiam, even unto Lasha. These are the sons of Ham, after their families, after their tongues, in their countries, and in their nations." *Genesis 10:15-20*

Nimrod is most famous for his part in building the Tower of Babylon which was built between the Tigress and Euphrates rivers. In my opinion, it appears that all of Canaan's family had been victimized by the second eruption of the fallen angels because both Cush and his son Nimrod were said by many ancient cultures as being giants. As stated earlier, according to many occult traditions, Cush's oldest daughter Semiramis became a prostitute and eventually had sex with her own father. Semiramis, thus became the mother, and half-sister of Nimrod, and later became his wife. One might accurately call Semiramis the original "Whore of Babylon." According to the Jewish historian Flavius Josephus, Cush also had 11 other sons besides Nimrod, Sidonius, Arudeus, Arudeus, Eueus, Chetteus, Jebuseus, Amorreus, Gergesus, Eudeus, Sineus, Samareus. *The Works of Flavious Josephus, Antiquities* 1.6.2. One of Cush's sons Amorreus, was the founding father of the Amorrhites, or Amorites, some of which are mentioned in the *Bible* as being giants. **"But thou shalt utterly destroy them; namely, the Hittites, and the Amorites, the Canaanites, and the Perizzites, the Hivites, and the Jebusites, seven nations much more numerous than thou art, and stronger than thou."** *Deuteronomy 7:1*

Many ancient pagan cultures referred to the various sons of Cush as gods with supernatural powers and intellect, who functioned as trance mediums and were the first to establish what today is known as Paganism. The Septuagint plainly states that Nimrod was a giant: **"And Chus** (Cush) **begot Nebrod** (Nimrod): **he began to be a giant upon the earth. He was a giant hunter before the Lord God; therefore they say, As Nebrod the giant hunter before the Lord."** *Septuagint Genesis 10:8-9 LXX*

Historian and author Rob Skiba, states in his book *Archon Invasion* **"According to many ancient cultures, Nimrod was often depicted as a mighty warrior giant and possibly a hunter and subduer of giants as well. In fact, giants are even said to have helped him build the Tower of Babel. An Arabic manuscript found at Baalbek says: After the flood, when Nimrod reigned over Lebanon, he sent giants to rebuild the fortress of Baalbek, which was so named in honor of Baal, the god of the Moabites and worshipers of the Sun."**

Babylon's religion was polytheism, which is the worship of nearly seventy gods and goddesses, represented as constellations, and the sun and moon as separate gods in their own right. Some of the better known gods were Ningirsu, An, Anshar, Kishar, Ki, Enlil, Utu, Inanna, Beletili, Ea, Sin, Ninurta, Nergil, Ninlil, Ningal, Ninhursaga, Namtar, Nabu, Ereshkigal, Dumuzi, Marduk, Esagila, Sarpanitu, Sarpanit, Sarpanitu, Sarpanitum, Shamash, Nanna, Enki, and Ishtar. Likewise, in Egypt these same gods were worshiped through thirty successive dynasties by such names as Shu, Tefnet, Geb, Atum, Nut, Nephtys, Horus, Ankn, Anubis, Ammit, Aset, Thoth, Ausir, Set, Osiris, and Isis. The ancient Egyptians belived this was the period of time they had enjoyed a golden age of absolute perfection known as Zep Tepi, meaning "The First Time." From this grew all the ancient Mystery religions of Semiramis and Isis, which are, today, the origin of all Pagan forms of Witchcraft, and Anti-Christian religions, including Pseudo-Christian new-age religions. Many years after the Babylonian Empire was over-thrown by the Medo-Persion Empire, they continued the worship of the Sun and the Moon, in what became known as the Mysteries of Isis, and the religion known as Zoroastrianism. The Isis Cult, and the Zoroastrians both revered the brightest star in the sky, Sirius, as the secret power that energized the Sun. Some of the many pagan names for Cush down through history was Kush, Janice, Sem, Belus, Bel, Aithiopais, Aethiops, Hermes, Kissioi, and Mercury. Author Jeremy Auldaney, in his book *Mysteries of History Revealed Part 2*, states: **"Cush is known as Mercury the god of knowledge or enlightenment which is the meaning of the word gnostic or Illuminati. Mercury stones are Megalithic stones or mound sites were where they contacted the spirits of demons. Megalithic stones or phallic stones, which symbolized male genitals were Mercury's symbol."** Cush was widely known as Hermes by the Egyptians and the Assyrians which is their synonym for the Son of Ham. Author Ben Zhen, in his book *The Two Jerusalems* comments: **"Hermes was recognized as the author of pagan religious rites. In fact, the composition of Hermes is from 'Her' which in Chaldee is synonymous with Ham, 'The Burning One.' Hence, Ham is deified as the sun god. Furthermore, Mes' Eguptian is 'Ms' in the sence of 'to bring forth.' Thus, Hermes is the 'Son of Her or Ham' the burnt one."** When Aleister Crowley took over control of the cult known as the Hermedic Order of the Golden Dawn, it was a Luciferian order dedicated to the study and practice of pagan magic taught by Hermes, or Cush. It was Cush's son Nimrod, and his wife Semiramis, however who had the greatest influence on the ancient pagan world and were known by many different names in many different cultures down through time. In Babylon, Nimrod was worshiped as the Sun God, and who after marrying his mother, and half-sister Semiramis, declared her to be the Goddess of Heaven, and of the Crescent Moon. In predominately Protestant countries such as the United States of America, Semiramis is usually portrayed as Columbia, the Goddess of Libertas, or Liberty, as depicted in our Statue of Liberty. Libertas was always considered to be the matron-goddess of prostitutes. She was also considered to be the matron-goddess of emigrants, or migrants. In predominately Catholic countries, she is usually depicted as the Goddess Mother, or simply as the Madonna with her child Tammuz at her breast. The Freemasons who designed and built the Statue of Liberty, knew that her true identity was the "Mother of all Harlots." Some of Nimrod's other names down through the years were Apollo, Apollyon, Abaddon,

Gilgimesh, Ninurta, Ninus, Ra, Abir, Apis, Brahma, Athom, Amun, Phtha, Osiris, Ausir, Lupercus, Marduc, Marduk, Merdock, Merodach, Ares, Pluto, Mercury, Nebo, Melqart, Eshmun, Bacchus, Dumuzi, Astalluhi, Mavor, Vulcan, Phoebus, Shamash, Sem, Tithonus, Molech, Belus, Bacchus, Bel, Ball, Bul, Teoti, Pan-Ku, Vishnu, Atlas, Moloch, Jason, Uranus, Ulysses, Sabazius, Mithras, Nebrod, Wodan, Odin, Helios, Assur, Enmerkar, Brama, Rebel, Rephan, Adon, Adonai, Coh, Adonis, Orion, Phoroneus, Liber, Oannes, Osiris, Saturn, Saturnalia, Sol, Deoius, Dionysos, Kronos, Cronis, Consus, Ala Mahozim, and Ceres. Nimrod's wife Semiramis, also known as the Mother of Heaven with her child in her arms, was also known down through time by many different names such as Isis, Isi, Ishta, Ishtar, Isha, Irene, Columbia, Demeter, Neith, Kali, Esther, Gaia, Athena, Shiva, Anahita, Belit, Anahita, Anat, Alliet, Aphrodite, Arbela, Hathor, Perseus, Aurora, Ariadne, Amarusia, Artemis, Ashta, Ashtar, Asherat, Asherah, Aset, Aspolia, Astarte, Ashtoreth, Rhea, Iacchus, Inanna, Beltis, Bona Dea, Lakshmi, Matuta, Mylitta, Moo, Rhea, Maut, Cybele, Ma Tsoopo, Fortuna, Liberttos, Leto, Themis, Clymene, Ceres, Cerelia, Proserpine, Venus, Virgo, Diy Pervati, Madonna, Diana, Devaki, Diana, Henz-O-Matsoopo, Coattlicue, Friig-Freyda, Dionusos, Dionysus and Baalat-Gebal. Semiramis' son Tammuz was also known by many different names throughout history such as Horis, Mars, Thammuz, Horis, Hercules, Dionysius, Yi, Quetzalcoatl, Harpok, Harsiese, Blader, Zues, Murguan, Orus, Adad, Bacchus, Plutus, Krishna, Iswara, Deoius, Deolus, Eros, Cupid, Zero, El Bar, Nimbus, Ninus, Phaethon, Dionysus, Krishna, Jupiter, Atis, Attalus, Sibyis, Thor, Janus, Matutinus, Mithra, Zoar, and Zoroaster. The all-time classic book *The Two Babylons* written over a hundred and fifty years ago by Alexander Hislop, remains still today the best book on the subject of the Babylonian Mysteries, created by Nimrod. In this book Alexander Hislop documents many of the names listed above as alternative names of Nimrod, Tammuz, and Semiramis. Hislop states: **"The Babylonians, in their popular religion, supremely worshipped a goddess Mother and a son, who was represented in pictures and in images as an infant or child in his mother's arms. From Babylon, this worship of the Mother and Child spread to the ends of the earth. In Egypt, the Mother and the Child were worshipped under the names of Isis and Osiris. In India, even to this day, as Isi and Iswara; In Asia, as Cybele and Deoius; in Pagan Rome, as Fortuna and Jupiter-puer, or Jupiter, the boy; in Greece, as Ceres, the Great Mother, with the babe at her breast, or as Irene, the goddess of peace, with the boy Plutus in her arms."**

After God came down to earth to see the city and tower of Babel, he confounded the language of its builders, thus scattering them abroad across the earth. Unfortunately mankind took with them the Mystery Religion of this Babylonian Trinity along with them and spread it throughout the earth. In Egypt this Babylonian trinity was known as Osiris, Horus, and Isis. In Greece the trinity was known as Zeus, Apollo, and Athena, while in India it was known as Brama, Vishnu, and Shiva. Later, during the time of the Roman Empire, this Babylonian Pagan Trinity was worshiped by all of Rome's' emperors, including Constantine, by such names as Jupiter, Mars, and Venus.

"Go to, let us go down, and there confound their language, that they may not understand one another's speech. So the Lord scattered them abroad from thence upon the face of all the earth; and they left off to build the city." *Genesis 11:7-8*

Again, Lucifer and all of his fallen angels were watching these events with great interest. Satan's plan was to replace the true story of the promised seed, given by God in the Garden of Eden with a counterfeit woman and child, which would become the basis of all pagan sun-worship throughout the world. Unfortunately this ancient form of paganism has come down to us today in the form of the Roman Catholic Church, yet most people today don't recognize it as paganism. As stated earlier, in Babylon the names of this trinity was Nimrods, Semiramis, and her child Tammuz, but in Egypt this trinity was better known as Osiris, Isis, and Horus. In 1799, in a place called Rosetta, Napoleon's solders stumbled across a large stone, now housed in the British Museum, known as the Rosetta Stone. The stone had the same words and symbols inscribed on it in three different languages which included Egyptian hieroglyphics. By matching the Greek words to the hieroglyphics, scholars were able to translate many new Egyptian symbols and inscriptions. Because of the Rosetta Stone, the Egyptian version of the trinity story was by far the best documented from ancient history, thus I shall now briefly relay the Egyptian version first. In the beginning, known as the First Time, Nut (Heaven) and Geb (Earth) procreated and gave birth to two brothers, Osiris and Seth, and two sisters, Isis and Nephthys. Osiris was given all the fertile land of Egypt. Osiris sometimes took on the form of a bull, which somehow gave him power over the Nile River which watered the soil that brought forth the corn, the fruit and the flowers. Osiris became so popular, and powerful that he became a threat to the powerful Sun-God Ra. Isis was given power over rain, and over all the other bodies of water other than the Nile River. Isis's breath gave life to all plants and animals, and her breast-milk nourished all the creatures on earth. Sometimes Isis took on the form of a tree, a star or a cow. Seth, Osiris's younger jealous brother, ruled over the deserts and loved to scorch all of Osiris' fertile fields with scorching heat. Sometimes Seth would take on the appearance of a donkey, a crocodile, or a hippopotamus. Isis' younger sister Nephthys, ruled over the darkness, as opposed to Isis, who ruled over the light. Isis is sometimes depicted with light beams emanating from her head, and holding a torch, such as seen on the Statue of Liberty. Nephthys loved the dark or waning moon, thus she was known as the invisible one. Isis loved the crescent new moon and the full moon, thus she was known as the visible one. When all four grew to adulthood, Isis married her brother Osiris and Nephthys married her brother Seth. Osiris taught the people how to hunt and how to plough and irrigate their fields so as to plant fruit trees and grains which they could make into bread. Osiris and Isis together taught the art of civilization by giving the people laws in order to bring order and the principle of justice to their lives. Isis is sometimes depicted holding a set of scrolls, or tablets of laws in her arms, again, just as depicted in the Statue of Liberty. Osiris traveled over all the earth teaching the principles of civilization and was often gone a long time, leaving Isis in charge, watching over the land. Seth was jealous of Osiris and disliked his brother's principles of order and civilization, and was never happy when Osiris returned home, thus he conspired with seventy-two (a powerful occult number) of his friends to kill Osiris. Seth built a magnificently decorated chest just big enough to hold the body of Osiris and then threw a lavish party. Seth promised to give the chest to the person who fit in it the best, thus after several of Seth's friends tried laying in it, Osiris laid down in it. Immediately the seventy-two conspirators rushed forward, slammed down the lid and nailed it shut. Later Seth killed Osiris, and cut his body up into fourteen pieces, then hid his severed penis. After being told that the chest holding Osiris's dead body had been dumped into the Nile River and carried out to sea, Isis was heart-broken, and went into mourning. Later some children came and told Isis they had found the chest on the shore of Byblos in Phoenicia, entangled in the roots of a tamarisk tree. The chest was in the possession of the Queen of Byblos, thus because Isis' breastmilk was known for nourishing all creatures, the Queen of Byblos sent for her and asked Isis to nurse her own baby boy. After caring for the queen's baby, Isis then asked for the chest containing Osiris' body, which was granted her. Isis then quickly loaded it on a boat and sailed it back to Egypt. When she was sure no one was looking, Isis opened the chest and found Osiris's penis was missing, thus she constructed another one out of gold in the form of an obelisk. Osiris' penis from that time forward was always considered a symbol of resurrection from death, thus it was used by American freemasons as a pattern for the Washington Monument, which they built near the west end of the National Mall. Today this masonic inspired obelisk faces Washington's Capital Building, which has a nineteen foot high statue of Isis, or Semiramis (see back cover), atop its dome. After restoring Osiris' penis, Isis then kissed the body of her dead husband. Suddenly Isis was transformed into a great bird with giant wings which created a mighty wind which temporarily breathed life back into her husband's body, thus the two immediately made love, and she then conceived her son Horus. The occult power released by this sex act is revealed to us by Tomas Horn, in his book Apollyon Rising, who states: **"Through such imitative sex, the Dome and the Obelisk become 'energy receivers' capable of assimilating Ra's essence from the rays of the sun, which in turn drew forth the 'seed' of the underworld Osiris. The seed of the dead deity would, according to the supernaturalism, transmit upward from out of the underworld through the base (testes) of the Obelisk and magically ejaculate from the tower's head into the womb (Dome) of Isis. In this way, Osiris could be 'born again' or reincarnated as Horus over and over (the same deity that Horus in flesh is Osiris in the underworld)."** According to ancient occult beliefs, Washington's reflecting pool serves as the transferring point where these magical powers are released into the city. General Albert Pike, one of the leading authorities on freemasonry said that Isis and Osiris represented both the active and passive principals of the universe, commonly symbolized by the generative parts of a man and woman. The all-seeing eye of Horus/Osiris on the unfinished pyramid on the front of America's Great Seal represents Lucifer's power over America to bring about a New World Order, in order to control the whole world. At the time of America's Revolutionary War with England, most Americans considered themselves to be Christians, but the Masons who later designed and built Washington D.C., designed, built, and decorated it with hundreds of pagan monuments and statues, which can be seen throughout its street and intersections. The three-story design of Washington's Capital Building, was patterned by the Masons, after the Great Pyramid of Giza, which they believe to be the actual grave-site of Osiris. The Great Pyramid of Giza was built with three main chambers to facilitate the Pharaoh's transformation into Osiris, thus the three-story Capital Building was constructed inside, in three parts, the Tomb, the Crypt, and the Rotunda, which is capped by the buildings dome. The ancient story of Isis and Osiris, continues as Isis hid in the chest that had previously held her husband's body until she had given birth to her son Horus. In a different version of the same story, Isis hid Osiris's dead body in the chest and hid it in the tall reeds of the marshes in a city named Busiris, in the Delta, and then also hid herself. One night, while hunting wild boar on a full moon, Seth, stumbled onto the chest and found it still held the body of his brother Osiris. Seth ripped off the lid, and in a jealous rage cut the dead body of Osiris into fourteen pieces, and spread them throughout Egypt. When Isis heard of this she and her sister Nephthys searched for all the pieces if Osiris' body, but only found thirteen pieces. Osiris's penis was missing because it had been swallowed by a fish, thus Isis, with the magical wisdom of Thoth, made a copy of the missing penis, in the form of an obelisk and then reassembled the body. With the help of Anubis, the Jackal-headed god, Isis performed a magical ritual over the body of Osiris using the magical Egyptian Cross known as the Ankh (see Google), thus Osiris immediately came back to life. From that time forward Thoth was considered the keeper of records. He was also associated with the arts, science, astronomy, and writing in the form of hieroglyphs. From that time forward Anubis was always considered to be the god of embalming. Anubis was the original god of the dead before Osiris removed him from that position and took his place. After that, Abubis was seen as one of the many sons of Osiris, whose job it was to escort dead souls into the underworld. There, Anubis would place the heart of the dead soul on the Scale of Justice to determine who was righteous or evil. Those who were found to be evil were feed to the god Ammit. Osiris, who had adopted the Ankh (a cross with a round handle) as his cross, and symbol of his resurrection, then was considered the chief god of the dead, and the judge of the underworld. Osiris took his Ankh with him and then went down to rule the underworld just as he had earlier ruled over the earth. Every night Ra, the sun-god came to awaken Osiris just at the time everyone else on earth was going to sleep. Remember, Osiris, was the Egyptian name for Nimrod, but the Hebrews called him Abaddon, and the Greeks called Nimrod by the name Apollyon. Is it possible that the *Book of Revelation* reveals to us that the ruler of the underworld is actually

Nimrod? **"And they had a king over them, which is the angel of the bottomless pit, whose name in the Hebrew tongue is Abaddon, but in the Greek tongue hath his name Apollyon."** *Revelation 9:11*

Isis then hurried back to Horus who was still hiding in the reeds to protect him from Seth who was now looking to kill him. Isis then seeks the help of the god Thoth, who comes to her help in a flying disk, or flying saucer. Thoth said to Isis: **"O Isis, thou goddess, thou glorious one. I have come this day in the Boat of the Celestial Disk from the place where it was yesterday. I have come from the skies to save the child for his mother."** Thoth protected Horus, thus when he grew up to be a man he began to look for Seth to avenge the dismemberment of his father's body. When Horus finally found Seth, they fought for three days, but Horus could not kill him. Thoth, who knew the difference between good and evil finally intervened and told them that force could not make a wrong right. Isis and Horus then appealed to the Court of the Law, told their story, and appealed for justice. When the court called Seth to give an account, he was not believed and was found guilty by the god Atum-Ra. The verdict passed was that Seth must forever carry the boat of the Sun as it crosses the sky. He must overcome the Serpent of Darkness who tries to recapture the Sun each night. Horus, the falcon-god, then climbed the steps of his father's throne and took his place ruling over the upperworld, while Osiris continued to rule over the underworld as the new chief god of the dead. Osiris then sat on his throne in the Hall of Truth with his forty-two demon-judges and greeted the souls of the dead after their hearts were weighed against the Feather of Truth. If their hearts were as light as a feather he welcomed them into his underworld kingdom. There, they spend eternity in the heavenly fields of Yaru, the grain fields of Osiris, where food was abundant, and life was easy. If they are found lacking in venture, they were condemned to an eternity of hunger and thirst. If the soul was judged by Osiris's forty-two demon judges to having been an outright, blatant sinner, it was cut to pieces and fed to Ammit, the detestable little goddess that ate souls. Then, every year when the Nile River flooded, and the land was renewed and covered with flowers, the Egyptian people always remembered the resurrection of Osiris. From that time forward Osiris was always associated with the yearly death and resurrection of nature, especially of grains and crops in the field, especially barley. From that time forward, the Pharaohs were always thought to be the son of the sun-god Ra, and the reincarnation of the falcon-headed god Horus during their lifetime, but after their death, they were thought to become the reincarnation of Osiris, the god of the underworld. After a period of time ruling over the underworld, Osiris's spirit was thought by the Egyptians to have been resurrected out of the underworld, and onto one of the three stars, Alnt, Alnilam, and Mintaka, which make up Orion's Belt. Today in National Harbor Maryland, not far from Washington D.C., there is a giant statue, known as The Awakening (see You Tube), of what I personally believe to be a depiction of Nimrod, or Osiris, coming up out of the underworld. The three stats of Orion's Belt are all extremely bright and are grouped away from other bright stars, which make their line pattern all the more obvious. To the Greeks they represented the belt or girdle of the giant hunter Orion, whose constellation is one of the largest to be seen in the night sky. Osisir's body was then supposedly taken and buried in the Great Pyramid at Geza, which was built by the giants to house his body, until he is once again is resurrected. This is why the three pyramids at Giza are laid out in the same staggered alignment, as the three stars of Orion's Belt. The various Babylonian versions of this same story were somewhat different from each other, and from the Egyptian version. In the various Babylonian versions of this story, one of them states that after one of Nimrod's extended trips abroad, he returns to find Semiramis pregnant with Tammuz. Before he can expose and divorce her, she has Nimrod killed and cuts his body into fourteen pieces, then hides each piece separately. In order to preserve her position as the Queen of Babylon, Semiramis tells her subjects that she went looking for the various pieces of Osiris' body, but could not find his penis. As in the Egyptian version, Isis told the story of how she formed a penis out of a golden obelisk and magically resurrected Osiris into becoming the Sun God. Semiramis told her subjects that she had been impregnated by Osiris before he ascended to heaven as the Sun God. Thus, Tammuz was presented as the son of Osiris, a virtual reincarnation of his father the Sun God. After Tammuz grows to manhood he demands to be crowned king, but Semiramis refuses to give up her power as queen. Tammuz eventually stabs, and kills his mother, whereupon she ascends to the heavens and forever reigns as the Moon Goddess. Tammuz then reigns as king for forty years until he is killed in a hunting accident by a wild boar. From that time forward, the Egyptian Pharaohs were seen as the extension of the spirit of Osiris, especially during the festival of Opet, which was held each year at the temple of Luxor, where the Pharaoh supposedly entered the holy womb-temple and then was transformed into the living deity, the son of Amun-Ra and Osiris, which was Horus, or Tammuz. In Egypt the site of this yearly festival was held at the temple of Amun-Ra at Karnak, the largest religious structure ever built on earth. In the Bible, we are told that many Israeli men and women worshipped Tammuz as the Sun God in the Temple for forty days, a day for each year of Tammuz's reign, as part of their Baal worship. **"Then he brought me to the door of the gate of the Lord's house which was toward the north; and, behold, there sat women weeping for Tammuz. Then said he to me, Hast thou seen this, O son of man? Turn thee yet again, and thou shalt see greater abominations than these. And he brought me into the inner court of the Lord's house, and, behold, at the door of the temple of the Lord, between the porch and the alter, were about five and twenty men, with their backs toward the temple of the Lord, and their faces toward the east; and they worshipped the Sun toward the east."** *Ezekiel 8:14-16*

Today there are two very visible statues of Semiramis in America but they are not known to the general public by that name. When visitors come to Washington D.C. to visit our capital's monuments, they are looking at a great, possibly the ultimate conspiracy, because they do not understand the pagan treditions of what they are seeing. The nineteen foot cast iron statue of Semiramis, setting atop our Capital Building's dome, is commonly known by the public as the Goddess of Columbia, or the Goddess of Liberty. The other statue of Semiramis sets near the entrance of New York's harbor and is known by the public as the Statue of Liberty, both inspired, and built by the Masons. The Statue of Liberty was built and dedicated on October 28th, 1886, by a mason named Gustave Eiffel, the man who later built the Eiffel Tower. However it was Frederic Auguste Bartholdi, a French Freemason who first sculpted and designed the statue of Liberty, based on the Roman Goddess Libertas. The truth that few Americans have ever been told is that Libertas was just another name for Semiramis. Bartholdi originally never intended his statue to be built in America, but rather in Egypt. Offering the Statue of Libertas to American Freemasons was an afterthought, when the Egyptian Freemasons could not raise the money to build a proper base to hold it. After the Egyptian Freemasons said thanks, but no thanks, Bartholdi secretly put out feelers to France, England, and American freemasons to see if there was any interest whereupon both France and American freemasons responded. Another secret the American people have never been told is the fact that Bartholdi was a secret member of an Egyptian Isis cult, dedicated to the study and practice of ancient Egyptian occult-ism. When designing the statue, Bartholdi had made a trip from France to Egypt, inspecting statues and artwork depicting both Isis and Semiramis. The people of Egypt would gladly have accepted a statue based on Isis, or Semiramis, but the Christians of America would never have contributed to a statue depicting Isis or Semiramis, the wife of Nimrod, thus she was sold to America as Libertas, the Goddess of Liberty.

Chapter 4

The Ancient Book of Jasher

The ancient *Book of Jasher* is more than 3, 500 years old and was written approximately the same time Moses wrote the *Book of Genesis,* and the *Book of Exodus.* This book was never considered to be inspired by God or to be part of the cannon of scripture but was **mentioned by name twice in the Old Testament,** and referenced once in the *New Testament.* **"Then spake Joshua to the Lord in the day when the Lord delivered up the Amorites before the children of Israel, and he said in the sight of Israel, Sun, stand still upon Gibeon; and thou, Moon, in the valley of Ajalon. And the sun stood still, and the moon stayed, until the people had avenged themselves upon their enemies. Is not this written in the Book of Jasher? So the sun stood still in the midst of heaven, and hasted not to go dawn about a whole day. And there was no day like that before it or after it that the Lord hearkened unto the voice of a man: for the Lord fought for Israel."** *Joshua 10:12-14*

"And Joshua said in the sight of all the people, Sun stand thou still upon Gibeon, and thou moon in the valley of Ajalon, until the nation shall have revenged itself upon its enemies. And the sun stood stillmidst of the heavens, and it stood still six and thirty moments, and the moon also stood still and hastened not to go down a whole day. And there was no day like that before it or after it that the Lord harkened to the voice of a man, for the Lord fought for Israel." *Jasher 88:63-64*

The *Book of Jasher* is mentioned a second time in the *Old Testament* when David mourned over the death of Saul. "And David lamented with this lamentation over Saul and over Jonathan his son. Also he bade them teach the children of Judah the use of the bow: behold it is written in book of Jasher." *II Samuel 1:17-18*

"Only teach thy sons the use of the bow and all weapons of war, in order that they may fight the battles of their brother who will rule over his enemies" *Jasher 56:9*

The *Book of Jasher* is referenced in the *New Testament* by Paul, when he names Jannes and Jambres as standing against Moses. Their names were never mentioned in the Old Testament, thus Paul could only have learned their names from the *Book of Jasher*. "Now as Jannes and Jambres withstood Moses, so do these also resist the truth: men of corrupt minds, reprobate concerning the faith." *II Timothy 3:8*

"And when they had gone Pharaoh sent for Balaam the magician and to Jannes and to Jambres his sons, and to all the magicians and conjurors and cancellors which belonged to the king, and they all came and sat before the king." *Jasher 79:27*

After Noah's Flood, the *Book of Jasher* tells us that Nimrod, with the help of three families began the construction of the Tower of Babel. "And all these people, and all the families divided themselves in three parts; the first said, 'We will ascend into heaven and fight against him;' the second said 'We will ascend into heaven and place our own gods there to serve them;' and the third part said, 'We will ascend to heaven and strike him with bows and spears.' And God knew all their works and evil thoughts, and He saw the city and the tower which they were building." *Jasher 9:26*

This Book also gives us some insight into the teachings of Nimrod concerning the crossbreeding of plants and animals, which possibly included the practice of bestially, both of which angered God. "Then the sons of men began teaching the mixture of animals of one species with the other, in order wherewith to provoke the Lord." *Jasher 4:18*

The following is an excerpt from the eleventh chapter of the *Book of Jasher*. "In the fifteenth year of the life of Abram son of Terah, Abram came forth from the house of Noah, and went to his father's house. And Abram knew the Lord, and he went in his ways and instructions, and the Lord his God was with him.

And Terah his father was in those days, still captain of the host of King Nimrod, and he still followed strange gods. And Abram came to his father's house and saw twelve gods standing there in their temples, and the anger of Abram was kindled when he saw these images in his father's house.

And Abram said, As the Lord liveth these images shall not remain in my father's house; so shall the Lord who created me do unto me if in three days' time I do not break them all. And Abram went from them, and his anger burned within him. And Abram hastened and went from the chamber to his father's outer court, and he found his father sitting in the court, and all his servants with him, and Abram came and sit before him.

And Abram asked his father, saying, Father, tell me where is God who created heaven and earth, and all the sons of men upon the earth, and who created thee and me? And Terah answered his son Abram and said, Behold those who created us are all with us in the house.

And Abram said to his father, My lord, shew them to me I pray thee; and Terah brought Abram into the chamber of the inner court, and Abram saw, and behold the whole room was full of gods of wood and stone, twelve great images and other less than they without number.

And Terah said to his son, Behold these are they which made all thou seest upon the earth, and which created me and thee, and all mankind.

And Terah bowed down to his god's and he then went away from them, and Abram, his son, went away with him. And when Abram had gone from them he went to his mother and sat before her, and he said to his mother, Behold, my father has shown me those who made heaven and earth, and all the sons of men.

Now, therefore, hasten and fetch a kid from the flock, and make of it savory meat that I may bring it to my father's gods as an offering for them to eat; perhaps I may thereby become acceptable to them. And his mother did so, and she fetched a kid, and made savory meat thereof, and brought it to Abram, and Abram took the savory meat from his mother and brought it before his father's gods, and he drew nigh to them that they might eat; and Terah his father did not know of it.

And Abram saw on the day when he was setting amongst them, that they had no voice, no hearing, no motion, and not one of them could stretch forth his hand to eat. And Abram mocked them, and said, Surely the savory meat that I prepared has not pleased them, or perhaps it was too little for them, and for that reason they would not eat; therefore tomorrow I will prepare fresh savory meat, better and more plentiful than this, in order that I may see the result.

And it was on the next day that Abram directed his mother concerning the savory meat, and his mother rose and fetched three fine kids from the flock, and she made of them some excellent savory meat, such as her son was fond of, and she gave it to her son Abram; and Terah his father did not know of it.

And Abram took the savory meat from his mother, and brought it before his father's gods into the chamber; and he became nigh unto them that they might eat, and he placed it before them, and Abram sat before them all day, thinking perhaps they might eat. And Abram viewed them, and Behold they had neither voice nor hearing, nor did one of them stretch forth his hand to the meat to eat.

And in the evening of that day in the house Abram was clothed with the spirit of God. And he called out and said, Wo unto my father and his wicked generation, whose hearts are all inclined to vanity, who serve these idols of wood and stone which can neither eat, smell, hear nor speak, who have mouths without speech, eyes without sight, ears without hearing, hands without feeling, and legs which cannot move; like them are those that made them and that trust them.

And when Abram saw all these things his anger was kindled against his father, and he hastened and took a hatchet in his hand, and came into the chamber of the gods, and he broke all his father's gods. And when he had done breaking the images, he placed the hatchet in the hand of the great god which was there before them, and he went out; and Terah his father came home, for he had heard at the door the sound of the striking of the hatchet; so Terah came into the house to know what this was about.

And Terah, having heard the noise of the hatchet in the room of images, ran to the room to the images, and he met Abram going out. And Terah entered the room and found all the idols fallen down and broken, and the hatchet in the hand of the largest, which was not broken, and the savory meat which Abram his son had made was still before them.

And when Terah saw this his anger was greatly kindled and he hastened to Abram. And he found Abram his son still sitting in the house; and said, what is this work thou hast done to my gods? And Abram answered Terah and he said, not so my lord, for I brought savory meat before them, and when I came nigh to them with the meat, they all at once stretched forth their hands to eat before the great one had put forth his hand to eat.

And the large one saw their works before him that they did and his anger was violently kindled against them, and he went and took the hatchet that was in the house and came to them and broke them all, and behold the hatchet is yet in his hand as thou seest. And Terah's anger was kindled against his son Abram, when he spoke this; and Terah said to Abram his son in his anger, what is this tale that thou hast told?

Thou speakest lies to me. Is there in these gods spirits, souls or power to do all thou hast told me? Are they not wood and stone, and have I not myself made them, and canst thou speak such lies, saying that the large god that was with them smote them? It is thou that didst place the hatchet in his hands, and then sayest he smote them all.

And Abram answered his father and said to him, and how canst thou then serve these idols in whom there is no power to do anything? Can those idols in which thou trust deliver thee? Can they hear thy prayers when thou callest upon them? Can they deliver thee from the hands of thy enemies, that thou shouldst serve wood and stone which can neither speak nor hear?

And now surly it is not good for thee nor for the sons of men that are connected with thee, to do these things; are you so silly, so foolish or so short of understanding that you will serve wood and stone, and do after this manner? And forget the Lord God who made heaven and earth, and who created you in the earth, and thereby bring a great evil upon your souls in this matter by serving stone and wood?

Did not our father sin days of old sin in this matter, and the Lord God of the universe brought the waters of the flood upon them and destroyed the whole earth? And how can you continue to do this and serve gods of wood and stone, who cannot hear, or speak, or deliver you from oppression, thereby bringing down the anger of the God of the universe upon you?

Now therefore my father refrain from this, and bring not evil upon thy soul and the souls of thy household. And Abram hastened and sprang from before his father, and took the hatchet from his father's largest idol, with which Abram broke it and ran away. And Terah, seeing all that Abram had done, hastened to go from his house, and he went to the king and came before Nimrod and stood before him and he bowed down to the king; and the king said, what dost thou want?

And he said, I beseech thee my lord, to hear me. Now fifty years back a child was born to me, and thus has he done to my gods and thus has spoken; and now therefore, my lord and king, send for him that he may come before thee, and judge him according to the law, that we may be delivered from his evil.

And the king sent three men of his servants, and they went and brought Abram before the king. And Nimrod and all his princes and servants sat, and Terah sat also before them. And the king said to Abram, what is this thou hast done to thy father's gods? And Abram answered the king in the words he spoke to his father, and said, the large god that was with them did to them what thou hast heard.

And the king said to Abram, have they power to speak and eat and do as thou hast said? And Abram answered the king if there be no power in them why serv them and cause the sons of men to err through thy follies? Dost thou imagine that they can deliver thee or do anything small or great, that thou shouldst serv them? And why wilt thou not serv the God of the whole universe, who created thee and in whose power it is to kill and keep alive? O foolish, simple, and ignorant king, woe unto thee forever,

I thought thou wouldst teach thy servants the upright way, but thou hast not done this, but hast filled the whole earth with thy sins and the sins of thy people who have followed thy ways. Dost thou not know, or hast thou not heard, that this evil which thou doest, our ancestors sinned therein in days of old, and the eternal God brought the waters of the flood upon them and destroyed them all, and destroyed the whole earth on their account?

And wilt thou and thy people rise up now and do like unto this work, in order to bring down the anger of the Lord God of the universe, and to bring evil upon thee and thee whole earth? Now therefore put away this evil deed which thou doest, and serve the God of the universe, as thy soul is in his hands, and then it will be well with thee.

And if thy wicked heart will not hearken to my words to cause thee to forsake thy evil ways, and to serve the eternal God, then wilt thou die in shame in the latter days, thou, thy people and all who are connected with thee, hearing thy words or walking in thy evil ways. And when Abram had ceased speaking before the king and princes, Abram lifted up his eyes to the heavens, and he said, the Lord seeth all the wicked and he will judge them." *Jasher 11:13-61*

Before leaving the Book of Jasher, I would like to point out that it tells the story of how Esau decapitated the head of Nimrod in an ambush. "And Nimrod and two of his men that were with him came to the place where they were, when Esau started suddenly from his lurking place, and drew his sword, and hastened and ran to Nimrod and cut off his head.

And Esau fought a desperate fight with the two men that were with Nimrod, and then they called out to him, Esau turned to them and smote them to death with his sword.

All of the mighty men of Nimrod, who had left him to go to the wilderness, heard the cry as a distance, and they knew the voice of those two men, and they ran to know the cause of it, when they found their king and the two men that were with him lying dead in the wilderness." *Jasher 27:7-9*

Chapter 5

The Ancient Book of Enoch

"And God looked upon the earth, and, behold, it was corrupt; for all flesh had corrupted his way upon the earth. And God said unto Noah, the end of all flesh is come before me; for the earth is filled with violence through them; and behold, I will destroy them with the earth." *Genesis 6:12-13*

As Jesus sat on the Mount of Olives with his disciples, he gave them the following sign of the last days: "But as the days of Noah were, so shall also the coming of the Son of man be. For as in the days that were before the flood they were eating and drinking, marrying and giving in marriage, until the day that Noah entered into the ark, and knew not until the flood came, and took them all away; so shall also the coming of the Son of man be." *Matthew 24:37-39*

America was once a Christian nation, but sadly within my own lifetime, I have watched its moral and spiritual decline has happened to the point that, like God, my spirit is grieved. As a former pastor, I often wonder how we as Christian leaders have been so cowardly and fearful, as to allow our churches to become so insignificant and weak. Most of our old line denominations, which were once such a blessing to this nation, have turned into spiritual country clubs, having no concept of spiritual warfare. There is no urgency in these spiritual country clubs to be looking for Christ's return because now the *Bible* is so seldom taught. There is a lot of eating, and drinking going on in our churches, and a lot of marriages, but sadly, little true *Bible* teaching. The word of God is our strength, thus without teachers, we have no spiritual strength to affect our culture and society. Jesus warned us repeatedly not to be deceived, yet our government controlled media deceives us on a daily basis. When both of our political parties lie to us, we are often left to wonder whose side our Government is really on. When our ever increasing tax dollars are secretly used to fund the killing of our own babies, and the selling of their organs to China, can judgement be far off.

The violence and pornography produced by Hollywood has so demoralized our children, and our churches that we are often shocked to find our children's values are no longer our values. Sexual deviance, and homosexual lifestyles are portrayed for our children so see on prime time television, and for the most part, our churches remain silent. Again, can judgement be far off? No! it is not far off for we can see its affects all around us in our churches, schools, governments, and our economy. Gangs openly sell drugs and rule our major cities, often with more firepower than our police forces can muster. Every week hundreds of drug dealers are shot or knifed in drug deals gone bad while our police forces are often afraid to even enter these neighborhoods for fear of being shot themselves or being charged with murder if someone is killed by them. How can there be an end to this perversion, anarchy, and violence? **"And the earth also was corrupt before God, and the earth was filled with violence. And God looked upon the earth, and, behold, it was corrupt; for all flesh had corrupted his way upon the earth. And God said to Noah, the end of all flesh is come before me; for the earth is filled with violence through them; and behold, I will destroy them with the earth."** *Genesis 6:11-13*

Although the *Book of Enoch* is not a part of our Protestant Scriptures, it is quoted from in the New Testament by Jude, the half-brother of Jesus. "And Enoch also, the seventh from Adam, prophesied of these, saying, **Behold, the Lord cometh with ten thousands of his saints."** *Jude: 14*

Jude was giving a direct quote from the second chapter of the *Book of Enoch* which fully states: **"Behold, he comes with ten thousands of his saints, to execute judgment upon them, and destroy the wicked, and reprove all the carnal for everything which the sinful and ungodly have done, and committed against him."** *Enoch 2:1*

In the *Epistle of Jude* we also have a reference to the fallen angels who gave themselves over to fornication, and went after strange flesh. These fallen angels are today held in darkness, reserved for the fiery judgements that awaits them. **"And the angels which kept not their first estate, but left their own habitation, he hath reserved in everlasting chains under darkness unto the judgement of the great day. Even as Sodom and Gomorrah, and the cities about them in lack manner, giving themselves over to fornication, and going after strange flesh, are set forth for an example, suffering the vengeance of eternal fire."** *Jude:6-7*

Many early church fathers such as Clement, Methodius, Origen, Felix, Commodianus, and Ambrose, believed the *Book of Enoch* to be inspired by God. Because the *Book of Enoch* reveals that God allowed Enoch to return to earth after being caught up to heaven, some early church fathers such as Filastrius saw this as a form of reincarnation, despite the fact that Enoch is said to have never died. Rabbi Simeon ben Jochai, in the second century, went so far as to place a curse upon any Jew owning, or even reading a copy of the *Book of Enoch*. Julius Africanus (200-245) taught that the Sons of God referred not to angels but to the righteous sons of Seth who fell in a moral sense when they took the unrighteous daughters of Cain as wives. Jerome (348-420) compared the *Book of Enoch* to the Luciferian Manichean's *Book of the Giants,* which is quite similar. Fragments of both the *Book of the Giants*, and the *Book of Enoch* were found among the Dead Sea Scrolls. Jerome stated: **"Just as the Manicheans say that souls desire human bodies to be united in human pleasure, do not they who say that angels desire bodies, or the daughters of men, seem to you to be saying the same thing as the Manicheans?** The Manicheans were the disciples of a Jewish Luciferian named Mani, who believed in reincarnation, and wrote several books including the *Book of the Giants*. Mani believed Lucifer was a good god, while Jehovah, the god of the Christians and Jews, was an evil god. For a detailed study of the Manicheans read my book *The Synagogue of Satan*, or my book *Lucifer's Children*. The axe finally fell when Augustine (354-430), who had himself once been a Manichean, sided with both Jerome and Africanus, when he taught that the Sons of God spoken of in *Genesis* referred to the righteous sons of Seth, who sinned when they married the daughters of Cain" Because of this the *Book of Enoch* was rejected by most of the early church fathers, and by many church councils, thus the book virtually disappeared for almost two thousand years. Today there are three entirely different versions of the *Book of Enoch*, sometimes referred to simply as 1st Enoch, 2nd Enoch, and 3rd Enoch. 1st Enoch is sometimes referred to as the *Ethiopian Book of Enoch*, which was written in an Ethiopian language known as Geez. The 2nd *Book of Enoch* is sometimes called the *Slovonic Book of Enoch*, which was discovered in 1886 by Professor Sokolov in the archives of the Belgrade Public Library. The 3rd *Book of Enoch* is often called the *Hebrew Book of Enoch,* which was written mostly in Hebrew, but has a few words written in Latin and Greek. **WARNING,** The Freemason's love this book because this third book teaches that Enoch, after being translated to heaven, was then transformed into Metatron, the most powerful of all the angels, such as Ruhiel, Ramiel, and Rashiel. The Freemasonns teach that Enoch's fleshly body was then turned into a flame of fire, with sparks flying in all directions. His eyelashes flashed lightning bolts, and his eyeballs resembling a flaming torch. From then on, all angels, both good and bad, had to obey him, thus the angels dressed him in a magnificent garment, and gave him a crown of righteousness, then seated him on a throne next to god. Obviously, there is much that is unscriptural in this third book, thus it deserves to be rejected. Today there are three very similar books known as the *Book of Giants*, the *Book of Parables*, and the *Book of the Watchers*. The version I will be quoting from is 1st Enoch, which is much older than the other two versions. This book was saved from obscurity by a Scottish explorer named James Bruce. In 1773 Bruce heard of surviving copies of the book in the hands of the Ethiopean Mizrahi Jews. Bruce quickly traveled to Ethiopia and managed to acquire three copies. In 1821, an Oxford trained Hebrew scholar named Richard Laurence translated the first English version of this book into one hundred and five chapters. In recent times New Age occultists like Erick von Daniken call the fallen angels spoken of by Enoch, by the name Anunnaki, and say they were not angels, but extraterrestrials from planets beyond our solar system. Whether you consider the *Book of Enoch* to be divinely inspired history, an uninspired secular record book, a Gnostic forgery, or simply esoteric mythology, we must not today consider it to be on the same level as the *Bible*. Still, I believe it will be interesting to give several quotes from the *Book of Enoch* in this chapter and let the reader determine if it is of any real value to our understanding of Noah's flood. The main thing that made the days of Noah unique from all other generations was the hybridization of both humans and animals by the fallen angels. The first chapter of the *Book of Enoch* informs the reader that his message is not for his generation but for a generation of God's elect, far into the future who are suffering in a time of great tribulation. **"I saw; that which will not take place in this generation, but in a generation which is to succeed at a distant period, on account of the elect."**

The *book of Enoch* also tells us that it was in the lifetime of his father Jared that Lucifer's fallen angels first appeared on earth on top of Mount Hermon, which is located on the border between Syria and Lebanon. Jared was born in 3544 BC, thus if Enoch's information is correct this incident happened some time later, probably around 3550 BC. Jared was 162 years old when Enoch was born, thus Enoch was born in 3382 BC, and was probably about 32 years old when the fallen angels rebelled and took human wives. "And it came to pass when the children of man had multiplied that in those days were

Then swore they all together and bound themselves by mutual imprecations upon it. And they were in all two hundred; who descended in the days of Jared on the summit of Mount Hermon, born unto them beautiful and comely daughters. And the Angels, the children of heaven, saw and lusted after them, and said to one another: Come, let us choose us wives from among the children of men and begat us children.

And Semjaza, who was their leader, said unto them: I fear ye will not indeed agree to do this deed, and I alones hall have to pay the penalty of a great sin. And they all answered him and said: Let us all sware an oath, and all bind ourselves by mutual imprecations not to abandon this plan but to do this thing.

and they called it Mount Hermon, because they had sworn and bound themselves by mutual imprecations upon it. And these are the names of their leaders: Semiazaz, their leader, Arakiba, Rameel, Kokabiel, Tamiel, Ramiel, Danel, Ezeqeel, Baraqial, Asael, Armaros, Batarel, Ananel, Zaqiel, Samsapeel, Satarel, Turel, Jomjael, Sariel. These were their chiefs of ten." *Book of Enoch 6:1-8*

The pollution of the earth caused by these fallen angels was both spiritual and physical as they contaminated the bloodlines of both humans and animals. If the *Book of Enoch* can be believed, bestiality was part of the sinful lifestyles of these fallen angels. This truth is also to be found in the *Book of Jubilees.* "And after this they sinned against the beasts and birds, and all that moveth and walketh on the earth: and much blood was shed on the earth, and every imagination and desire of men imagined vaniety and evil continually." *Jubilees 7:24*

The most important thing God saw in Noah was the fact that his family's bloodline had not been polluted by the fallen angels. "And the Lord said, I will destroy man whom I have created from the face of the earth; both man, and beast, and the creeping thing, and the fowls of the air; for it repenteth me that I have made them. But Noah found grace in the eyes of the Lord. These are the generations of Noah: Noah was a just man and perfect in his generations (towldah-genealogy), and Noah walked with God." *Genesis 6:7-9*

Noah's family may have been the only family left on earth with an un-polluted bloodline, thus, if this was true, the promised seed of the woman would one day have to come from one of his children. Noah's family may also have been the only family on earth not to have been spiritually pollut-ed by the false teachings of the fallen angels concerning the heavenly-gos-pel told by the constellations concerning the promised seed of the woman. **"And Azazel taught men to make swards, and knives, and shields, and brestplates, and made known to them the meals and the art of work-ing them, and bracelets, and ointments, and the use of antimony, and the beautifying of the eyelids, and all kinds of costly stones, and all colouring tinctures. And there arose much godlessness, and they com-mitted fornication, and they were led astray, and became corrupt in all their ways. Semjaza taught enchantments and root-cuttings, Armaros the resolving of enchantments, Baraqijal astrology, Kobabel the con-stellations, Ezeqeel the knowledge of the clouds, Araziel the signs of the earth, Shamsiel the signs of the sun and Sariel the course of the moon. And, as men perished, they cried, and their cry went up to heaven."** *Book of Enoch 8:1-4*

As men began to cry out to God, the fallen angels realized that their sins would eventually catch up to them, and that judgement would soon be pronounced upon them. The angels then approached the righteous Enoch to intercede to God for themselves, and to beg for mercy for their children the Nephilim. However, the answer they got back from God, was not the answer they wanted to hear. **"And I Enoch was blessing the Lord of majes-ty and the King of the ages, and lo! The Watchers called me---Enoch the scribe---and said to me: 'Enoch, thou scribe of righteousness, go declair to the Watchers of the heaven who have left the high heaven, the holy eternal place, and have defiled themselves with women, and have done as the children of earth do, and have taken unto themselves wives. Ye have wrought great destruction on the earth. And ye shall have no peace nor forgiveness of sin: and inasmuch as they delight themselves in their children, The murder of their beloved ones shall they see, and over the destruction of their children shall they lament, and shall make supplica-tion unto eternity, but mercy and peace shall ye not attain."** *Enoch 10:3-8*

Enoch had a son named Methuselah who lived to be 969 years old. When Methuselah was 187 years old he had a son named Lamech, who at the age of 182, had a son named Noah, who was born in 2948 BC. Again, if the *Book of Enoch* can be believed Noah was warned of a coming judgement, and that there would be a flood by an angel named Uriel. **"Then said the Most High, the Holy and Great One spake, and sent Uriel to the son of Lamech, and said to him: Go to Noah and tell him in my name "hide thyself" and reveal to him the end that is approaching: that the whole earth will be destroyed, and a deluge is about to come upon the whole Earth, and will destroy all that is on it. And now instruct him that he may escape and his seed maybe preserved for all the generations of the world."** *Book of Enoch 10:1-3*

If the angel Uriel really did warn Noah of a coming flood, did he also instruct Noah concerning the building of the ark, or of its proper demotions? In the New Testament we are told that some, but not all of the fallen angels, which left heaven, are today held inside the Earth, reserved in a place of darkness, called Tartarus until their day of fiery judgement, when they will be cast into the lake of fire.. **"For God did not spare angels when they had sinned, but hurled them down to Tartarus consigned them to caves of darkness, keeping them in readiness for judgment."** *II Peter 2:4* WNT

"And again the Lord said to Raphael: bind Azazel hand and foot, and cast him into the darkness; and make an opening in the desert, which is in Dudael, and cast him therein. And on the day of great judgment he shall be cast into the fire. And the whole Earth has been corrupted through the works that were taught by Azazel: to him ascribe all sin. And to Gabriel said the Lord: Proceed against the bastards and the reprobates, and against the children of fornication and the children of the Watchers from amongst men and cause them to go forth; send them one against the other that they may destroy each other in battle, for length of days shall they not have. And to the Lord said Michael: Go, bind Semjaza and his associates who have united themselves with women so as to have defiled themselves with them in all their uncleanness. In those days they shall be led off to the abyss of fire; to the torment and the prison in which they shall be confined forever." *Book of Enoch 10:4-14*

In the light of the coming judgement stated above, the fallen angels again petition Enoch for help. In both the fifteenth and sixteenth chapters of the *Book of Enoch,* he is asked by the fallen angels to again intercede to God, this time by way of a petition. Because Enoch was so loved by God, they again hoped Enoch's intercession might at least lessen their eternal sentence. Enoch then reads their petition and immediately falls asleep. In his sleep Enoch has a vision of God who instructs him to give the following message to the fallen angels: **"Then addressing me, He spoke and said, Hear, neither be afraid, O righteous Enoch, thou scribe of righteousness: approach hither, and hear my voice, Go say to the watchers of heaven, who have sent thee to intercede for them: You should intercede for men, and not men for you.** *Book of Enoch 15:1*

Although both demons and evil spirits are often mentioned in both the *Old Testament,* and the *New Testament,* nowhere in the *Bible* are we ever told about their origin. When and where did they come from? One of the things this author found most interesting, the *Book of Enoch* provides us with this answer.

"Wherefore have you left the high, holy and eternal Heaven, which endures forever, and have lain with women, and have defiled yourselves with the daughters of men and taken to yourselves wives, and done like the children of Earth, and begotten Giant sons. And though ye were holy, spiritual (beings) **living the eternal life you have defiled yourselves with the blood of women, and have begotten** (children) **with the blood of flesh and blood as those who die and perish.**

And now, the giants, who are produced from the spirit and flesh, shall be called evil spirits (demons) **upon the Earth, and on the Earth shall be their dwelling. And the spirits of the giants afflict, oppress, destroy, attack, do battle and work destruction on the Earth, and cause trouble: they take no food, but nevertheless hunger and thirst, and cause offinces. And now as to the watchers who have sent thee to intercede for them, who have been aforetime in Heaven** (say to them): **You have been in Heaven, but all the mysteries had not yet been revealed to you, and you knew worthless ones, and these in the hardness of your hearts you have made known to the women, and through these mysteries women and men work much evil on Earth. Say to them therefore: You have no peace."** *Book of Enoch 15:2-16:4*

Chapter 6

The Roots of Paganism

After Noah's Flood the world was again plunged into the depths of idolatry and paganism, mostly, as stated previously, because of the influence of Noah's son Ham, and his descendants. The following list is just a few of the names used for Nimrod, Semiramis, and Tammuz, in various cultures, and countries throughout the world. In Egypt Nimrod was called Osiris, his wife Semiramis was called Isis, and their son Tammuz was called Horus. In Assyria Nimrod was called Assur or Ninus, his wife was called Ishtar or Beltis, and their son was called Hercules. In Persia Nimrod was called Mithra, his wife was called Anahita, and their son was called Tammuz. In Phoenicia Nimrod was called El, his wife was called Astarte, and their son was called Backus. In the land of Shinar Nimrod was called Belus, his wife was called Rhea, or Ishtar, and their son was called Tammuz. In Greece Nimrod was called Helios or Zeus, his wife was called Artemis or Aphrodite, and their son was called Dionysius. In Rome Nimrod was called Apollo or Jupiter, his wife was called Cybele or Diana, and their son was called Attis. In India Nimrod was known as Vishnu, his wife was known as Isi or Devaki, and their son was called Krishna. In Mexico Nimrod was called Teoti, his wife was called Coattlicue, and their son was called Quetzalcoatl. In China Nimrod was called Pan-Ku, his wife was called Heng-O-Matsoopo, and their son was called Yi. In Scandinavia Nimrod was usually called Odin, his wife was called Friig-Freyda, and their son was called Blader. On the Island of Crete Nimrod was called Cronus, his wife was called Rhea, and their son was called Zeus, or Jupiter. Throughout Palestine, the *Old Testament* usually refers to Nimrod by the names Belus, Bel, or Baal, his wife was called Ashtoreth, and their son was called Tammuz. The ridiculous story I am about to relate to you next is the basis of what the ancients called the "Old Wisdom" or the "Old Religion," and, after it had spread throughout the entire world, it was later called the "Mystery Religions." Author Alexander Hislop, in his classic book The Two Babylons states: **"All who have paid the least attention to the literature of Greece, Egypt,**

Phoenicia, or Rome are aware of the place which the "Mysteries" occupied in these countries, and that, whatever circumstantial diversities there might be, in all essential respects these "Mysteries" in the different countries were the same." This ancient fertility religion was revived in Europe, in the middle-ages during the Italian Renaissance, and again later during what became known as the Enlightenment. This ancient religion is alive today in America in a slightly differently form, in what we now call the counter-culture pagan inspired "New Age Movement." In the ancient world the names of this ancient pagan religion were changed from one geographic region to another, but the basic theme of the following myth remained the same. The following is the Greek version of this ancient pagan-myth. The ancient Greeks believed that these beings caused everything that happened on earth. Every rain shower, every flash of lightning, every fall harvest, every sunrise, and sunset were all caused by one or more of these gods and goddesses. In the beginning, before there was an earth, sky, sea, or people, there was only a mass of emptiness, darkness and confusion. Somehow out of this chaos, emerged Gaea, or "Mother Earth." After Gaea was born, she later gave birth to a son named Uranus, or Ouranos, thus she became both his mother and wife. Uranus so loved Mother Earth's flowers and trees, he made rain to continually fall on her until eventually rivers, lakes, and oceans began to form. Gaea, and Uranus, who had now become known as Father Heaven, had sex each day, and ultimately gave birth to multiple children which was called Hekatoncheires. Her first three sons looked like monsters with several heads, and multiple arms and hands. Her second three sons were very violent gigantic Cyclopes, with one eye in the middle of their forehead. Mother Earth then gave birth to six giant sons, and six giant daughters, which were very civilized, and wise, which they called Titans. Father Heaven could not stand the sight of his six ugly sons, so one day he secretly threw them in a dark hole called Tartaros, located under the earth, thus Mother Earth began to cry. When she found out where Father Heaven had hid her children, she made magical sickles as weapons for her children. She then told her six Titan sons: "Kill your cruel father, go to that dark hole and bring back my children." Cronus, or Kronos, was called the "Horned one, and was the king of the Cyclops." Kronos was the bravest, and strongest of the Titans, who along with Prometheus, and Epimetheus, led the attack against their father, but only succeeded in wounded him. After releasing his brothers, Cronus/Kronos, was made the ruler of both heaven and earth, and then made his sister Rhea, his wife and queen.

Power eventually changed Cronus until he became much like his father and once again imprisoned the unruly Cyclopes, and his monster brothers in that same dark hole. Mother Earth was again enraged, but this time said nothing, knowing Rhea would eventually bear a son that would be destined to overthrow his father. Cronus knew also that one of his sons was destined to overthrow him as king and takeover his place as ruler over all the gods. Therefore Cronus devoured Rhea's first five children: Hestia, Demeter, Hera, Hades, and Poseidon. They were all eaten as soon as they were born, before they could grow up and become powerful. Determined to save her next child, as soon as her sixth child Zeus was born, Rhea hid him. She then wrapped a stone in a baby blanket and presented it to Cronus to eat, saying: "Do whatever you wish with him." Rhea then took Zeus to Mother Earth, who hid the baby in a cave on the island of Crete. There, Zeus was fed ambrosia and nectar, the food and drink of the gods, and quickly grew tall and strong. There, also, Zeus grew up far from the influence of his wicked father, however Cronus eventually learned that Zeus was still alive, and went looking for him. When Zeus learned that Cronus was seeking to eat him as he had his brothers and sisters, he turned himself into a serpent, thus Cronus could not find him. When Zeus was fully grown Mother Earth helped him to return back to his mother Rhea, whereupon the two hatched a plan to make Zeus a servant within Cronus' household. Rhea then concocted a poison and told Zeus to pour it into his father's drink, thus after drinking it, Cronus became violently ill and vomited up the stone along with Zeus's brothers. They, together then made a pact to make Zeus their leader in making war against Cronus. For ten long years a war raged between Zeus and Atlas, who by that time had taken over control of the Titan's from Cronus. In the end, two of the Titan brothers, Prometheus, and Epimetheus, who had earlier helped Cronus, switched sides and loyalties. This made both sides virtually equal in strength so that neither side could win the battle. Gaea, or Mother Earth then intervened, telling Zeus: "Return to the dark hole under the earth and retrieve the Cyclopes, and their monster brothers to help you." After finding the dark hole of Tartarus, Zeus descended into its depths, and after killing all the guards, freed all its prisoners. After being freed, the Cyclopes gave Zeus the use of thunderbolts to use as a weapon against Cronus and the Titans. Another Cyclopes gave Zeus's brother Hades, who the Romans called Pluto, a magic "Helmet of Darkness." A third Cyclopes gave Zeus's brother Poseidon, who the Romans called Neptune, a sharp three-pronged trident. Zeus, Poseidon, and Hades, all thanked the Cyclopes, then conspired together how they might use their new weapons to defeat Cronus, and Atlas. Hades put on the Helmet of Darkness, which made him invisible, then crept up behind Cronus and stole his weapons. Poseidon struck the ground with his trident, causing an earthquake. Cronus was terrified by the earthquake and became too frightened to fight back. When Zeus threw his thunderbolt, Cronus, Atlas, and all the rest of the Titan's fled in fear. Zeus and all his brothers and sisters punished all the Titan's except Prometheus and Epimetheus, who had switched loyalties and helped them. They captured Cronus and chained him in the dark hole of Tartarus. They then captured Atlas, and sentenced him to carry the whole sky on his shoulders forever. In order to peacefully settle the question of which of the three brothers should be the leader of the universe they then drew lots. Hades won the underworld, Poseidon won the sea, and Zeus was crowned lord of heaven and earth and became the leader of all the gods who supposedly resided on the snow-capped peak of Mount Olympus. Mount Olympus is in reality, a real mountain in Greece with its peak rising over 9,600 feet high. Here, supposedly, the pagan-gods were said to live with the same virtues and vises that humans would eventually be subject to. Here also Zeus lived with his wife Hera, who the Romans called Juno, his son Hermes, who the Romans called Mercury. Here also was Zeus's two daughters, Athena, who the Romans called Minerva, the goddess of wisdom, and Aphrodite, who the Romans called Venus, the goddess of love and beauty. Hera, the queen of the gods was Zeus' sister, and was tall and very beautiful, but could be extremely spiteful and vengeful if crossed. Her daughter Aphrodite was so beautiful that everyone that looked on her became her slave. Through the power of her magic girdle, Aphrodite's spell caused everyone to lose their wits and babble uncontrollably. Wherever she stepped, the sand turned to grass and flowers bloomed. Aphrodite's son, Eros, who the Romans called Cupid, the god of erotic-love, was a rascal, whose arrows caused the gods to fall in love with each other, no matter how much trouble it caused. Zeus's son Hermes, or Mercury, wearing his winged cap and sandals, was his father's messenger to the other gods and goddesses. Hermes was the patron god of thieves, gamblers, liars, and the guardian of travelers. Hermes kept a workshop on Olympus an there invented playing cards, astronomy, and the alphabet. The stage was now set for man to be created, thus Zeus, rewarded the two faithful and loyal Titan brothers, Prometheus and Epimetheus, the job of creating both man and animals on the earth. Epimetheus created all the animals on earth, while Prometheus created mankind in the likeness of the gods. Prometheus later got in trouble with Zeus when, with the help of the goddess Athena, he snuck into heaven and brought back fire to give to mankind, because they were often cold and hungry. Prometheus had first approached Zeus saying: "Man is at the mercy of the beasts and weather, and he eats his meat raw, because he has no fire." Zeus was aware of this problem, but he was unconcerned, saying: "I will not give them even a spark. No indeed! Why, if man had fire they might become strong and wise like ourselves, and after a while, they would drive us out of our kingdom. Let them shiver with cold and live like the beasts. It is best for them to be poor and ignorant, so that we Mighty Ones may thrive and be happy." Prometheus said nothing, but became more determined to give mankind the gift of fire, thus he ignored Zeus, and smuggled fire out of Mount Olympus to earth. Now with the use of fire Prometheus then taught man how to cook their food, to melt copper and iron to make metal tools to build their houses. He also taught them how to tame the sheep and cattle, how to plant and harvest crops, to use herbs for healing, and to understand the positions of the stars. As things on earth began to improve, Prometheus declared: "A new Golden Age shall come, brighter and better by far than the old." During this new Golden Age for mankind, Zeus was sexually driven and had children by many humans such as Europa, the daughter of King Agenor, of the city of Tyre, who also founded the city of Thebes. Their son was Minos, the great king of Crete. Minos fathered a daughter by Leda, the daughter of Thestious, king of Aetolia. She was the beautiful Helen, who became the wife of Menelaos, king of Sparta, and then was abducted by Prince Paris of Troy, which supposedly caused the Trojan War. Zeus took on the guise of Amphitryon, king of Thebes and secretly had sex with his wife Alkmene. Their son was Herakles, the hero who supposedly performed twelve famous "labors." Zeus also had a son with the imprisoned Danae, the daughter of Akrisios, the King of Argos. Their son was the hero Perseus, the demigod Hitler became so fascinated with. Zeus also fathered the Nine Muses (patronesses of the arts), Clio, Euterpe, Thailia, Melpoment, Terpsichore, Erato, Polyhymnia, Ourania, Qurania, and Calliope. Prometheus would later pay dearly for his rebellion to Zeus after it was learned it was he who had stolen the miracle of fire, and brought it to earth. After being given the gift of fire, back on earth, mankind began to act like the gods and goddesses, becoming vindictive, jealous, and envious of each other. Some wanted to be a king, while others just wanted to be rich. Instead of peace and safety, there was only war and starvation, thus Zeus becomes angry with mankind and then formed the Council of Nine to punish mankind. This council consisted of Apollo, Athena, Hera, Hermes, Poseidon, Aphrodite, Demeter, who the Romans called Ceres, Hephaestus, who the Romans called Vulcan, and, of course Zeus. Together, the council decided to destroy the human race by a flood, but first they would punish mankind. Zeus ordered his blacksmith son, Hephaestus, the son of Hera, to form a women even more beautiful than his daughter Aphrodite, with the attributes of charm, deceit, eloquence, and curiosity. The blacksmith took a lump of clay and then molded it into a beautiful, but lifeless body. Then said Zeus: "Come now, let us all give our best gifts to the woman." One goddess gave her a beautiful voice, another gave her good manners, another gave her a kind heart, another goddess gave her skills in many arts, while another goddess gave her the gift of curiosity. Zeus gave her the gift of life and then named her Pandora, which means "the all-gifted one." Pandora was so beautiful, and gifted that no one could help but love her, thus Zeus would use her as bait. Zeus' son Hermes brought Pandora to earth, then offered her to Prometheus' brother, the second loyal Titan, Epimetheus. With just one glance, Epimetheus could not help but fall in love with her, and took her as his wife. Pandora had brought to earth a beautiful golden box, supposedly full of many precious things, which Zeus had told her to carefully guard. Wise Athena, then warned Pandora, who had been given the gift of curiosity, saying: "Never, never open it, nor try to see what is inside." Every time Pandora looked at the box her curiosity grew and grew, until she could not resist opening it. Suddenly out of the box came ten thousand strange creatures bearing sickness, disease, pain, poverty, anger, hate, troubles, and sorrows, which up until that time humans had not known. Pandora then shrieked with fear saying: "What will now become of me, and what will become of all mankind?" Suddenly Pandora heard a tapping coming from inside the box which she had slammed shut. Pandora said: "Who is that inside the box?" The voice from within said: "Lift the lid again and you shall see!" Despite her curiosity Pandora replied: "No, she cried, I have had enough of lifting the lid. You are inside the box, and there you will stay. Ten thousand of your brothers and sisters are bringing misery to the world. Don't think I would be so foolish as to let you out to join them." I am not like those evil creatures said the voice from inside the box, and things are not as bad as you might think. Lift the lid again and I will show you. Pandora's curiosity became uncontrollable as she flung open the lid of the box and out came a beautiful winged creature with a golden glow which lit up the whole room. I am Hope, said the beautiful creature, and I will make amends for that swarm of evil creatures. Do not fear for we shall do well in spite of them all. Pandora then said: "Will you stay here with me forever?" Hope replied, "I will stay as long as you need me, but there will come times when you will think I have left the earth entirely, but again and again, in times of trouble, you will see the glimmer of my wings. Even the vengeance and wrath of Zeus cannot destroy me, or dim my glow. Never fear Pandora, for good thing await you. She then took Pandora by the hand and led her out into the world to bring hope, joy, and promise back into the earth." Nevertheless, when Prometheus learns of Zeus' vengeful plan to flood the earth, he told his son Deukalion to make an ark and take his wife Pyrrha on board. Ultimately the ark floated on the water for nine days and finally lands on Mount Parnassos, whereupon Deukalion disembarks and, in hopes of appeasing him, makes a sacrifice to Zeus. Eventually Zeus located, and captured Prometheus and has him chained to the topmost peak of the Caucasus Mountains, where he could not move hand or foot. Yet Prometheus quietly bore his humiliation, pain, and suffering without a groan, or asking for mercy and forgiveness. Ages passed and still he remained chained until one day a brave young warrior took pity on Prometheus, and despite Zeus's dreaded thunderbolts, broke the chains and freed him. "I knew you would come," said Prometheus to the young hero. But, please, tell me your name so that I may thank you, thus the young hero replied: "I am called Hercules." Again, one version or another of this same bazar myth spread far afield throughout the world until it came to dominate the thinking of the whole of mankind.

Chapter 7

The Roots of Witchcraft

All of these ridicules pagan-myths might have been considered just harmless bed-time stories, had they not been turned into the Mystery Religions, and used to control, and dominate the people of the ancient world. The practice of witchcraft, or Wicca goes all the way back to Nimrod, and the Tower of Babble, but it was not known by those names until much later. In just about all ancient pagan countries, and cultures, there arose two forms of paganism which I will briefly attempt to define in this chapter. These pagan traditions, and religions would later come up against the newly emerging first-century Church, thus all of the original apostles, except the Apostle John, would be martyred by their pagan followers. As stated earlier, not long after the death of Nimrod, Semiramis, and Tammuz, a global manifestation of goddess worship, and fertility cults appeared throughout the earth. This earth-goddess was called by many different names, but in almost every case she was worshiped as the earth-goddess of erotic-love and fertility, as in the case of the Roman Venus, or Aphrodite in Greece. In Phoenicia she was called Beruth, In Wales she was called Rhiannon, or Cerridwen, In Ireland she was called Anu, or Brighid. In Lithuania she was called Romuva, In Britain she was called Brigantia, In France she was called Liberttos, In Germany she was called Nerthus, in the Norse world she was called Freya, in the Celtic world she was called Brighid, or Morrigan. At this same time a second manifestation of paganism appeared throughout the world, which today is known by anthropologists as the religion of Animism, or Shamanism. In this ancient religion was the belief that all elements of the material world, both tangible, and intangible, were imbued, and connected to spirits. Wind, sky, fire, rivers, trees, rocks, mountains, animals, and even the planets, stars, and constellations, were all alike in that they could all be communicated with, and influenced by the spirit world. Spirit-guides could be summoned to act as mediators between these various animals, earthly elements, and the planets, stars, and constellations. Those who summoned these spirit-guides were called shamans, and oracles, who used herbs, drugs, and shamanistic trance techniques to travel to these elements, planets, and stars, and then communicate with their spirits. Animists, and Shamans even believe the earth itself is a living, breathing thing, with a spirit that can be communicated with. To become a Shaman usually requires the knowledge of how to read and interpret the various forms of divination, and magic. Most uninformed people think of magic as pulling rabbits out of hats, or turning ex-husbands into toads. Real "Spirit-Magic" requires a strenuous, and often dangerous initiation, which includes near starvation, thirst, and constant prayers, and learning how to properly combine various psychoactive and hallucinogenic plants. These plants are used to help the magician learn the secrets of guided-visualization, and astral-projection. Pagans believe genuine magic entails cooperation with the various spirits of gods and goddesses in order to gain supernatural power over other people. The novice shaman began their education into magic by learning how to perform mantra-meditations, and contact-rituals, in which they learn how to make incenses and oils to attract spirits that can be trusted. Magicians learn how to take water, milk, beer, and wine, to mead, and form small cakes, which are given to the spirits to placate, and pacify them. Many magicians, shamans, and oracles undergo a fertility initiation of death and rebirth in which spirits usher, and guide them out of their bodies to communicate with other spirits, in far-away places. Once they have mastered these techniques, the shamans then concentrates on their ability to enter into a prolonged shamanistic trance, with the help of hallucinogenic drugs. Shamans then travel deep into the forest where they hallucinate about having their internal organs removed, washed, and then reinserted. The worship of Apollo was promoted in several temples, throughout the ancient world, in such places as Dodona, Trophonius, Latona, Eleusis, and Delphi. The most famous of these was the Oracle of Delphi, located in the Greek city of Ddelphi, where a large temple, dedicated to Zeus, had been erected. There, Apollo, the seer-god, spoke through a prophetess, or temple-priestess, usually called a Pythoness, Pythia, or a Sibyl. According to their Greek tradition, the Pythoness, setting in a tripod of gold, over a fissure in the earth, became ecstatic after breathing in magic vapors, thus she began to prophecy. The Oracles could not prophecy unless they breathed in the magic vapors that arose from the rotting flesh of the dragon Python, which supposedly had been killed by Apollo. According to this tradition, Apollo climbed the side of Mount Parnassus, looking for the python who had stalked, and tried to eat his mother Dryads. Apollo drew his bow and struck the giant snake, but only wounded it. After finding it in a cave Apollo slew the serpent, after a long, and prolonged battle, whereupon, he skinned it, leaving the body to rot. Thus this rotting flesh gave inspiration to all the temple priests, and priestesses. The real story behind these so called magic vapors comes from the fact that shepherds tending their flocks of goats on the side of Mount Parness were amazed at the peculiar antics of their goats, after wandering close to a large chasm on its southwestern clefts. There really were noxious fumes that caused their animals to jump, dance about, and make strange sounds as if they were trying to talk to their shepherds. Later, when the shepherds ventured too close to this fissure, trying to learn the cause of this phenomenon, they too were seized with a type of prophetic ecstasy. Supposedly after one of these shepherds was so overcome by this ecstasy, they threw themselves headlong into the chasm, thus, its vapors from that time were considered to be magical. From that time forward virgin maidens were consecrated to the service of the oracles, and were called Phoebades, or Pythice, which constituted the famous order known as the Pythian Priesthood. The Pythia were paid to prophecy by kings and rulers from around the world, such as Alexander the Great, before waging a war. The Pythia often prophesied in a strange, and unfamiliar voice, thought to be that of Apollo himself. A similar Pagan Temple was located at Eleusis Greece, dedicated to one of Zeus' sisters, the pagan goddess Demeter, which simply means Barley-Mother. Another name for her is Ceres, from which we get our word cereal. She was the goddess of planting and harvesting grain. Demeter was celebrated as the Goddess of harvest, each year from September 17, to September 23, with a fertility ritual of death and rebirth. Orgies were a daily occurrence, along with the eating of barley cakes which had been laced with hallucinogenic drugs. Each year the Catholic Church celebrates the Virgin Mary, in her guise as "Our Lady of Sorrows," in September, at the very same time of year as the "Mysteries of Demeter." Part of the yearly Demeter Mystery ceremony had to do with Demeter's daughter Persephone, who had been kidnapped by Pluto, or Hades, the brother of Zeus, and god of the underworld. Demeter climbed into her chariot and sped to Olympus, where she confronted Zeus saying: our brother Hades has .stolen our daughter, give me justice! When Demeter demanded again that her daughter be set free, Zeus compromised and agreed only that she be freed two-thirds of the year to her mother, then return one-third of the year, during winter, to Hades in the underworld. The worship of Demeter first started with the Minoans on the Island of

Crete, in about 2000 B.C, then spread to Greece, where it continued until the first-century Church destroyed it. Each year, during the harvest, during the third week in September, people, from all around the Mediterranean, who were known as Mystery Aspirants, would gather in Athens. Then, together they would all paraded twenty miles out to the pagan temple, located in the little town of Eleusis. There, they waved stalks of barley in the air, after which they celebrated by having orgies which lasted all week. Eleusis was held as sacred because Demeter, supposedly had appeared there in person, ordering a temple dedicated to her to be built. Later, during the First-Century Church, the Apostle Paul's Gentile Church eventually came against such forms of sexual perversion, and divination practiced by temple-priestesses, until, by the third-century, almost all of these pagan temples had been abandoned. Historian and author Richard Cavendish, in his book Man, Myth, and Magic, states: **"Apollo....delivered his last oracle in the year 362 AD, to the physician of the Emperor Julian, the Byzantine ruler who tried to restore paganism after Christianity had become the official religion of the Byzantine Empire. 'Tell the King,' said the oracle, 'that the curiously built temple has fallen to the ground, that bright Apollo no longer has a roof over his head, or prophetic laurel, or babbling spring. Yes, even the murmuring water has dried up."**

In the *New Testament* we are given a perfect example of an Apollonian Sibyl In, in the city of Thyatira, who prophesied for profit. **"And it came to pass, as we went to prayer, a certain damsel possessed with a spirit of divination (of python), met us, which brought her masters much gain by soothsaying. The same followed Paul and us, and cried, saying, These men are the servants of the most high God, which shew unto us the way of salvation. And this she did many days. But Paul, being grieved, turned and said to the spirit, I command thee in the name of Jesus Christ to come out of her. And he came out the same hour. And when her masters saw that the hope of their gain was gone, they caught Paul and Silas and drew them into the marketplace unto the rulers. And brought them to the magistrates, saying, These men, being Jews, do exceedingly trouble our city."** *Acts 16:16-20*

In these out of body experiences, Shamans, and Oracles like the Pythia, and the Sibyls, were often asked to journey, outside their bodies, to seek an alliance with friendly or powerful spirits to help a person, or family. Shamans are also often hired to contact these same spirits in order to place curses on individuals, and families. After learning these techniques, spirits often spoke through these Shamans, thus, they were often respected as community leaders, guides, healers, and soul retrievers. Shamans believe sickness is often the result of a person's soul being stolen, or kidnapped, by a spirit, thus they are often hired to recapture that soul. These spirits often appear to the Shaman in the form of an animal, snake, or bird in order to teach him new and different techniques to cause him to be more powerful in the spirit world. The most successful Shamans were those who learned not to trust the spirits, thus they learned to trust only a few spirits (called family, or familiar spirits) whom they could safely alley themselves with. Shamans believe each day Father Sky comes together with Mother Earth, or Mother Nature, and together they fertilize the earth. These two forms of paganism grew together to form the strange witches-brew we now call witchcraft, or Wicca. Ancient goddess-worship, combined with ancient Shamanism, and the Oracles worshipped in pagan temples, together formed the foundation of the Old Religion. Generally speaking, in the western world, the Old Religion could be divided into two divisions, the masculine, represented by the sun, and the feminine, represented by the moon. In more modern times we can draw a distinction between the eastern pagan religions such as the Buddhists, Tantrists, Taoists, and Hindus, and the western pagan religions such as the Wiccans, Druids, Rosicrucians, Freemasons, Satanists, Luciferians, Jewish-Kabbalists, and the Roman Catholic Church. In the Wiccan Religion, Female Witches were often seen as the village wise-woman, midwife, and herbalist-doctors, thus they were often held in high esteem. The ancient Druids however were seen as the Celtic's priesthood, scientists, philosophers, and lawyers, all rolled into one, thus this is why Julius Caser, in his writings referred to them as men of science and great learning. Although Witches and Druids are very different from each other they have a few things in common such as their worship of nature-spirits, and the sun, moon, planets, and stars. Witches and Druids both gather together in group meetings, sometimes in cities, but generally out in the country in groves, and meadows, to perform various forms of magic, alchemy, sorcery, and soothsaying. Some of the larger groups buy land to make nature preserves where they build stone circles in order to perform their Mandala Rituals. A Mandalas is generally a large circle, or a five pointed pentagram, drawn on the ground in which spirits are both conjured and contained. These Mandala- spirits are often referred to as the 'Guardians of the Doors of Reality.' These guardian-spirits are thought to be the demigods that man will encounter after death, in the state of 'Bardo.' Both Witches, and Druids consider themselves as healers, capable of tapping into the magical life-force known as the Reiki, or Chakras. The Reiki, or Chakras are the energy field that controls the health, and balance of the human body, thus they can be opened or closed as needed for good health. When the body is out of balance, supposedly the Chakras are shut down and spiritual energy can't flow evenly throughout the body. Witches and Druids both perform rituals that send messages to their subconscious-minds, which supposedly adjusts, and balances out their Chakras. Both Witches and Druids also perform rituals based on the Sabbats, and the Esbats, which happen at various times of the year. Sabbats are related to the sun's 30-to31-day colander month, and occur at eight specific times of the year. Esbats, by contrast, are based on the cycles of the moon, and its 29.5-day lunar month. The Sabbat cycle consists of eight holidays, including the solstices, equinoxes, and four ancient Celtic festivals. Pagans all believe solstices, equinoxes, and various stages of the moon have a profound impact, and influence on each person on earth. Almost all pagans use Nimrod's Zodiac to mark the pathway of the sun through the constellations. The ancient system of measuring the year was based upon the equinoxes and the solstices. The new year always began with the vernal equinox, which is usually celebrated on March 21st with rejoicing to mark the moment when the sun passed northward by the equator, up the zodiacal arc. The summer solstice was usually celebrated on June 21st, when the sun reached its most northerly position, after which the sun begins to descend toward the equator. The fall equinox was usually celebrated on September 21st, as the sun continues its southbound descent. Finally, the winter solstice was usually celebrated on December 21st, as the sun reached its most southerly position. Almost all pagans believe there are thirteen fazes of the moon, each emanating a power that can be tapped, controlled, and directed. These yearly fazes of the moon are January's Wolf Moon, February's Storm Moon, March's Innocent Moon, April's Seed Moon, May's Hire Moon, June's Dyad Moon, July's Mead Moon, August's Corn Moon, September's Harvest Moon, October's Blood Moon, November's Snow Moon, December's Oak Moon, and the Blue Moon, which occurs in a calendar month with two full moons, which varies from year to year. Bothe Druids, and Witches practice magic in the form of omens, and divination, in their quest to gain control over nature-spirits, in order to dominate other people. Almost all pagans practice both white, and black magic, with the help of demonic spirits. The following is the main tenant that all Witches and Druids must agree to, in order to gain the help of their spirit-guides, in order to practice black-magic.

"The black-magician must agree that his demon, or spirit-guide, will serve him for his entire lifetime, whereupon after their death, the black-magician will become the life-long servant of his spirit guide." Although Witches are secretive about their beliefs and practices, they were never considered to be a secret society. Druids on the other hand always considered themselves to be a sun-worshiping secret society, based on all the old pagan gods Apollo, Mercury, Mars, Jupitar, and especially the Egyptian rites of Isis and Osiris. Thousands of years before the Christian Era, Druids were active in England, Ireland, and France. The word Druid comes from the Irish word *Drui,* which means "men of the oak trees." At certain seasons of the year, according to the positions of the sun, moon, and stars, the Arch-Druid climbed up into the oak trees to cut down mistletoe with a golden sickle consecrated only for that purpose. They then took the mistletoe and mixed it with mushrooms, truffles, and serpent's eggs to create tinctures, and medicines. The Druids were not only priests, but they also considered themselves to be physicians, sorcerers, scientists, and astrologers, with a deep understanding of Mother-Nature and her laws. The secret-societies, or mystery-schools of the Druids was broken down into three degrees, much in the same way as Blue Lodge Masonry. The first level was called the Ovate, or Ovydd, which was an honorary degree, given to men of high education, especially in medicine, astronomy, music, and poetry. The Ovates dressed in green, which was their sacred color of learning. The second degree as called the Bard, or Beirdd, who, dressed in sky-blue, which to them represented harmony and truth. The Bard were assigned the task of memorizing thousands of lines of sacred Druidic poetry. The third level was called the Derwyddon, whose job it was to minister to the needs of the people. Both Witches and Druids practice some form of numerology where they consign various meanings to different numbers and signs, which can be used to decode and encode secrets and mysteries. Pagan adepts of the mystery schools are often found looking for ways to incorporate numbers into their schemes, and to find meaning in what they see in numerical values in nature and in the universe as a whole. They often use numbers as a kind of language, as in the case of the Jewish Kabbalah. The lives of many Jews who follow the Kabbalah, are often completely controlled by these numbers.

Chapter 8

The Abrahamic Covenant

Satan and his fallen angels closely watched the families of the Children of Noah for they knew that from one of his three children would come the promised seed of the woman. They did not know until much later the promised seed-line would come through Shem. It was not made apparent to Satan until after a few generations of Shem's descendants produced a man named Abram, who was born about 350 years after Noah's Flood. When Abram was ninety nine years old God appeared to him and promised to be his God and greatly multiply his descendants. **"And Abram fell on his face: and God talked with him, saying, As for me, behold, my covenant is with thee, and thou shalt be a father of many nations. Neither shall thy name any more be called Abram, but thy name shall be Abraham; for a father of many nations have I made thee. And I will make thee exceeding fruitful, and I will make nations of thee, and kings shall come out of thee"** *Genesis 17:3-6*

Notice if you will, the covenant God made with Abraham was to be an everlasting covenant, which means it is still in existence today. Unlike the covenant God made about five hundred years later with Moses and the Children of Israel, Abraham's Covenant was an unconditional covenant. The only stipulation God made with Abraham was that he walk upright, and circumcise all his house and descendants. **"And God said unto Abraham, Thou shalt keep my covenant therefore, thou, and thy seed after thee in their generations. This is my covenant, which ye shall keep, between me and you and thy seed after thee. Every man child among you shall be circumcised."** *Genesis 17:9-10*

The covenant God made at Mount Sinai with Moses and the Children of Israel, also known as the National Covenant by theologians, was definitely conditional. If the Children of Israel kept God's laws they would be blessed in both the city (read the whole 26th chapter of *Leviticus*), and the field. If the Children of Israel would not keep God's commandments (read the whole 28th chapter of *Deuteronomy*), they would be cursed in both the city and in the field. Because it is impossible for God to lie, the Abrahamic Covenant was immutable, which means that it was unchangeable and unalterable, and sure to come to pass. **"For when God made promise to Abraham, because he could swear by no greater, he swore by himself, Saying, Surely blessing I will bless thee, and multiplying I will multiply thee."** *Hebrews 6:13-14*

It was also sure to come to pass in the lives of Abraham's descendants, for the covenant was made immutable to his children, Isaac and Jacob also. **"And I will establish my covenant between me and thee and thy seed after thee in their generations for an everlasting covenant, to be a God unto thee, and to thy seed after thee. And I will give unto thee, and to thy seed after thee, the land wherein thou art a stranger, all the land of Canaan, for an everlasting possession; and I will be their God."** *Genesis 17:7-8*

While Abraham's son Isaac was living in Padanaram, in the land of Syria, his wife Rebekah gave birth to twins, Esau, and Jacob. Years later, God appeared to Isaac and warned him not to travel into the land of Egypt, but rather to Gerar, in the land of the philistines, which God would show him. **"And the Lord appeared unto him (Isaac), and said, Go not down into Egypt; dwell in the land which I shall tell thee of. Sojourn in this land, and I will be with thee, and will bless thee; for unto thee, and to thy seed (Jacob), I will give all these countries, and I will perform the oath which I sware unto Abraham thy father. And I will make thy seed to multiply as the stars of heaven, and will give unto thy seed all these countries; and in thy seed shall all the nations of the earth be blessed."** *Genesis 26:2-4*

Just as God confirmed his Abrahamic Covenant to Isaac, and promised to make his seed as plentiful as the stars of heaven, he also later appeared to Jacob and ratified, and confirmed this same covenant to him. **"And , behold, the Lord stood above it (Jacob's Ladder), and said, I am the Lord God of Abraham thy father, and the God of Isaac: the land where on thou liest, to thee will I give it, and to thy seed."** *Genesis 28:13*

"And God appeared unto Jacob again, when he came out of Padanaram, and blessed him. And God said to him, thy name is Jacob: thy name shall not be called any more Jacob, but Israel shall be thy name: and he called his name Israel. And God said unto him, I am God Al-

mighty: be fruitful and multiply; a nation and company of nations shall be of thee, and kings shall come out of thy loins. And the land which I gave Abraham and Isaac, to thee I will give it, and to thy seed after thee will I give the land." *Genesis 35:9-12*

One of the many blessings God promised Abraham, Isaac, and Jacob was their children would be blessed abundantly, both financially and physically. This included so vast a number of decedents, that no man could possibly number them. "And I will make thy (Abraham's) seed as the dust of the earth: so that if a man can number the dust of the earth, then shall thy seed also be numbered." *Genesis 13:16*

"And thy (Jacob's) seed shall be as the dust of the earth, and thou shalt spread abroad to the west, and to the east, and to the north, and to the south: and in thee and in thy seed shall all the families of the earth be blessed." *Genesis 28:14*

"And he brought him (Abraham) forth abroad, and said, Look now toward heaven, and tell the stars, if thou be able to number them: and he said unto him, So shall thy seed be." *Genesis 15:5*

"And I will make thy (Isaac's) seed to multiply as the stars of heaven, and I will give unto thy seed all these countries; and in thy seed shall all the nations of the earth be blessed." *Genesis 26:4*

"That in blessing I will bless thee (Abraham), and in multiplying I will multiply thy seed as the stars of heaven, and as the sand which is upon the sea shore: and thy seed shall possess the gate of his enemies." *Genesis 22:17*

"And thou saidst, I will surely do thee good, and make thy (Jacob's) seed as the sand of the sea, which cannot be numbered for multitude." *Genesis 32:12*

Jacob had twelve sons by four different women, Leah, Rachel, Bilhah and Zilpah. Leah gave birth to Reuben, Simeon, Levi, Judah, Issachar and Zebulun, while Leah's handmaid Zilpah gave birth to Gad and Asher. Rachel gave birth to Joseph and Benjamin, while Rachel's handmaid Bilhah gave birth to Dan and Naphtali. Again, Satan and his fallen angels were watching closely to see which of these twelve sons the promised seed would come from. It was not long before they got their first clue as Jacob's favorite son Joseph was given a dream. **"And Joseph dreamed a dream, and he told it his brethren: and they hated him yet the more. And he said unto them, Hear, I pray you, this dream which I have dreamed. For, behold, we were binding sheaves in the field, and, lo, my sheaf arose, and also stood upright; and, behold, your sheaves stood round about, and made obeisance to my sheaf."** *Genesis 37:5-7*

Joseph being young and inexperienced did not exercise much tact when explaining this dream to his brothers. They already hated him for his coat of many colors which Jacob had given him, and now, this dream caused them to hate him even more. The thought of their younger brother ruling over all of them caused in them a root of jealousy that soon grew into murder. **"And he (Joseph) dreamed yet another dream, and told it his brethren, and said, Behold, I have dreamed a dream more; and, behold, the sun and the moon and the eleven stars made obeisance to me. And he told it to his father, and to his brethren: and his father rebuked him, and said unto him, what is this dream that thou hast dreamed? Shall I and thy mother and thy brethren indeed come to bow down ourselves to thee to the earth?"** *Genesis 37:9-10*

Although they had no way of knowing it at that time, but the answer to Israel's question would one day be a definite yes. After being sold into slavery by his brothers, Joseph ended up in Egypt as the number two man in power, second only to the Pharaoh. After Jacob's eldest son Reuben sinned against his father by sleeping with Bilhah, Rachel's handmaid, he was judged and lost his birthright blessing to the next oldest brother. **"Now the sons of Reuben the firstborn of Israel, for he was the first born; but, forasmuch as he defiled his father's bed, his birthright was given unto the sons of Joseph the son of Israel: and the genealogy is not to be reckoned after the birthright. For Judah prevailed above his brethren, and in him came the chief ruler; but the birthright was Joseph's."** *I Chronicles 5:1-2*

Joseph, as the eldest son of Jacob and Rachel, inherited his father's birthright blessing, which he would pass on to his two children. This made Joseph the head of the family in terms of both spiritual and secular affairs. Before Jacob died, Joseph brought his two sons Ephraim and Manasseh to his father Israel to receive their birthright blessing. Joseph was not happy with his father Israel because he crossed his hands and pronounced the greater blessing on Joseph's younger son Ephraim. **"And Israel stretched out his right hand, and laid it upon Ephraim's head, who was the younger, and his left hand upon Manasseh's head, guiding his hands wittingly; for Manasseh was the first born."** *Genesis 48:14*

Although Joseph protested, Israel refused to uncross his hands, saying though Manasseh would be great, his younger brother would be even greater. Israel further said Ephraim's descendants would become a multitude of nations. From that time forward the adoption of the two sons of Joseph into the Abrahamic Covenant was counted as the thirteenth tribe of Israel. It is these thirteen tribes of God's covenant people which we today commonly refer to as Jews. Although there are other groups of people who call themselves Jews, such as the Ashkenazi, and Sephardic Jews, these thirteen tribes of Israel are the only true covenant Jews. One of the promises God made to Abraham was that he would be a father of many nations with kings reigning over them. Strangely enough, God did not want the Jews to have an earthly king, but desired that all of their tribes would look to him for political and spiritual leadership. When the Jews first entered into the Promised Land they at first looked to God, but as they observed all the nations round about them, they demanded a king. **"Then all the elders of Israel gathered themselves together, and came to Samuel unto Ramah, And said unto him, Behold, thou art old, and thy sons walk not in thy ways: now make us a king to judge us like all the nations. But the thing displeased Samuel, when they said, Give us a king to judge us. And Samuel prayed unto the lord."** *I Samuel 8:4-6*

God replied that the Jews had not rejected Samuel but him, and then instructed Samuel to tell them all of the disadvantages of having an earthly king. Still the Jews persisted in having a king, thus God granted their demands and told Samuel to appoint them a king named Saul. Later Saul was removed because of sin, and God himself appointed David (of the tribe of Judah) as his replacement to rule over all thirteen tribes of Israel. Just as he had done earlier, God established an everlasting covenant with David that his throne and his descendants would rule over the Jews forever. **"But my mercy shall not depart away from him, as I took it from Saul, whom I put away before thee. And thine house and thy kingdom shall be established for ever before thee: thy throne shall be established forever."** *II Samuel 7:15-16*

"I have made a covenant with my chosen, I have sworn unto David my servant. Thy seed will I establish forever, and build up thy throne to all generations." *Psalms 89:3-4*

"As the host of heaven cannot be numbered, neither the sand of the sea measured: so will I multiply the seed of David my servant, and the Levites that minister unto me." *Jeremiah 33:22*

"And the angel said unto her, fear not, Mary: for thou hast found favor with God. And, behold, thou shalt conceive in thy womb, and bring forth a son, and shalt call his name Jesus. He shall be great, and shall be called the Son of the Highest: and the Lord God shall give unto him the throne of his father David. And he shall reign over the house of Jacob forever; and of his kingdom there shall be no end." *Luke 1:3*

Another promise God made to Abraham was that Abraham's seed would dwell in a land of their own, which the Israelites called their Promised Land. "Sojoune in this land, and I will be with thee, and will bless thee; for unto thee, and unto thy seed, I will give all these countries, and I will perform the oath which I sware unto Abraham thy father." *Genesis 26:3*

The *Bible* speaks of both a Covenant people, and a Promised Land as part of the Abrahamic Covenant. When God made this covenant with Abraham he was first told that ten different tribes were currently living in the land which God would ultimately give to Abraham's descendants: "In the same day the Lord made a covenant with Abram, saying, unto thy seed have I given this land, from the river of Egypt (Nile River) unto the great river Euphrates. The Kenites, and the Kenizzites, and the Kadmonites, and the Hittites, and the Perizzites, and the Rephaims. And the Amorites, and the Canaanites, and the Girgashites, and the Jebusites." *Genesis 15:18-21*

The Kadmonites, and the Kennizites appear to have disappeared by the time Moses entered into the Promised Land. The Kenites, and Kenizzites, as mentioned earlier, are mentioned eight times in the *Old Testament* and are described as definitely having at least some giants in their ranks. When God heard the cries of his people in Egypt, he commissioned Moses to return to Egypt to deliver his people. Moses was then told they would be given a land flowing with milk and honey, but there were still six groups of giants that would have to be destroyed. **"And I am come down to deliver them out of the land of the Egyptians, and to bring them up out of that land into a good land and a large, unto a land flowing with milk and honey; unto the place of the Canaanites, and the Hittites, and the Amorites, and the Perizzites, and the Hivites, and the Jebusites."** *Exodus 3:8*

On the day Israel was to pass over the Jordan River into their Promised Land, God warned both Moses and the Israelites they were going to face the giants. **"Hear, O Israel: Thou art to pass over Jordan this day, to go in to possess nations greater and mightier than thyself, cities great and fenced up to heaven. A people great and tall, the children of the Anakims, whom thou knowest, and of whom thou hast heard say, Who can stand before the children of Anak."** *Deuteronomy 9:1-2*

Knowing that the Israelites are going to be tempted to fear these giants once they see their size, God assures them he will be the one who will defeat them as a consuming fire. **"Understand therefore this day, that the Lord thy god is he which goeth over before thee; as a consuming fie he shall destroy them, and he shall bring them down before thy face: so shalt thou drive them out, and destroy them quickly, as the Lord hath said unto thee."** *Deuteronomy 9:3*

God then warned the Israelites that after he had given them the victory, they should not be tempted to fall into pride, thinking their victory was won by their own puny strength. God then reminded them that it was not because of their righteousness, but because of the wickedness of the giants that God would destroy them. **"Speak not thou in thine heart, after that the Lord thy God hath cast them out from before thee, saying, For my righteousness the Lord hath brought me in to possess this land: but for the wickedness of these nations the Lord thy God doth drive them out from before thee.**

Not for thy righteousness, or for the uprightness of thine heart, dost thou go to possess their land: but for the wickedness of these nations the Lord thy God doth drive them out from before thee, and that he may perform the word which the Lord sware unto thy fathers Abraham, Isaac, and Jacob." *Deuteronomy 9:4-5*

God then informs Moses and the Israelites that their Promised Land is nothing like the desert land they have just left behind in Egypt, but a mountainous land with lots of watered green grass fields, and an abundance of milk and honey. But to possess it they must be strong in faith, and be very courageous. "And that ye may prolong your days in the land, which the Lord sware unto your fathers to give unto them and to their seed, a land that floweth with milk and honey. For the land, whither thou goest in to possess it, is not as the land of Egypt, from whence ye come out, where thou sowest thy seed, and wateredst it with thy foot, as a garden of herbs. But the land, whither ye go to possess it, is a land of hills and valleys, and drinketh water of the rain of heaven. " *Deuteronomy 11:9-11*

Again, God warns Moses and the Israelites they must be careful to love and serve the Lord with all their heart and soul and not turn aside to worship all the false gods of the Land of Canaan. If they will obey and serve the Lord their land will have an abundance of rain and will produce corn, wine, and olive oil. "I will give you the rain of your land in his due season, the first rain and the latter rain, that thou mayest gather in corn, and thy wine, and thine oil. And I will send grass in thy fields for thy cattle, that thou mayest eat and be full. Take heed to yourselves, that your heart be not deceived, and ye turn aside, and serve other gods, and worship them." *Deuteronomy 11:14-16*

God repeatedly warns the Israelites they must destroy every giant tribe including every man, woman, and child. They are repeatedly warned not to be deceived into inquiring, or following after any of the false gods of the various giant tribes. God hated the abominable religious practices of these various giant tribes, especially the worship of the fertility god Moloch which involved the sacrifice of their own children. "Take heed to thyself that thou be not snared by following them (the giants), after that they be destroyed from before thee; and that thou inquire not after their gods, saying, How did these nations serve their gods? Even so shall I do likewise. Thou shalt not do so unto the Lord thy God: for every abomination to the Lord, which he hateth, have they done unto their gods; for even their sons and their daughters they have burnt in the fire to their gods." *Deuteronomy 13:30-31*

This was not a suggestion but a firm command for after entering into the Promised Land, any form of idolatry would carry a death sentence. No pity was to be shown, even if your friend, father, brother, wife, or children were guilty, you had to cast the first stone. "Thou shalt not consent unto him, nor harken unto him; neither shall thine eye pity him, neither shalt thou spare, neither shalt thou conceal him. But thou shalt surely kill him; thine hand shall be first upon him to put him to death, and afterwards the hand of all the people." *Deuteronomy 13:8-9*

This death sentence not only applied to individuals, but could also apply to a whole city. If the city leaders were found to be guilty of idolatry, every person in that city was to be cut down with the sword. Even the cattle were to be put to the sword, and the city, and all its contents were to be completely burned and never rebuilt. **"Then shalt thou inquire, and make search, and ask diligently; and, behold, if it be truth, and the thing (idolatry) certain, that such abominations is wrought among you. Thou shalt surely smite the inhabitants of that city with the edge of the sword, destroying it utterly, and all that is therein, and the cattle thereof, with the edge of the sword."** *Deuteronomy 13:14-15*

Because a majority of the Israelites murmured against Moses and Aaron in the desert of Zin, by saying why have you brought us into this wilderness, that we and our cattle should die here? Why did you make us come up out of Egypt, only to bring us into this evil place with no grain, figs, or water? Moses, after being told to speak to the rock, disobeyed God, when he struck the rock which followed them in the desert and provided them with water. Moses' punishment would be that he was to see the Promised Land from atop Mount Nebo, but he would not enter into it. **"And Moses lifted up his hand, and with his rod he smote the rock twice: and the water came out abundantly, and the congregation drank, and their beasts also. And the Lord spake unto Moses and Aaron, Because ye believed me not, to sanctify me in the eyesof the children of Israel, therefore ye shall not bring this congregation into the land which I have given them."** *Genesis 20:11-12*

After forty years of aimlessly roaming around in the wilderness, the Children of Israel were finally instructed by God to cross over the Jordan and possess their Promised Land, however Moses and Aaron would not be with them. They were strictly warned however not to spare any of the inhabitants so as not to learn or practice any of their abominable ways.

"When the Lord thy God shall bring thee into the land whither thou goest to possess it, and hath cast out many nations before thee, the

Hittites, and the Girgashites, and the Amorites, and the Canaanites, and the Perizzites, and the Hivites, and the Jebusites, seven nations greater and mightier than thou. And when the Lord thy God shall deliver them before thee; thou shall smite them, and utterly destroy them; thou shalt make no covenant with them, nor shew mercy unto them." *Deuteronomy 7:1-2*

"But of the cities of these people, which the Lord thy God doth give thee for an inheritance, thou shall save alive nothing that breatheth. But thou shall utterly destroy them; namely, the Hittites, and the Amorites, the Canaanites, and the Perizzites, the Hivites, and the Jebusites; as the Lord thy God hath commanded thee.

That they teach you not to do after all their abominations, which they have done unto their gods; so should ye sin against the Lord your God." *Deuteronomy 20:16-18*

When the original twelve Israelite spies entered into the Promised Land they saw something they had only heard about back in Egypt. Egyptian mythology was filled with stories about the giants, as later were the mythologies of both Greece and Rome. Despite the vast abundance of food in the land, when they first came face to face with the giants the majority of the spies lost all interest in fighting these seemingly undefeatable supernatural beings. **"And there we saw the giants, the sons of Anak, which come of the giants** (Nephilim): **and we were in our own sight as grasshoppers, and so we were in their sight"** *Numbers 13:33*

In all there were possibly nine major groups of giants and several smaller groups such as the Avvites, Geshurites, Sidonians, Rephaites, and Gibeonites mentioned in the *Old Testament*. In alphabetical order the nine major groups were the Amalekites, Amorites, Canaanites, Girgashites, Hittites, Hivites, Jebusites, Perizzites and Philistines. Just how tall some of these giants really were is debatable depending on what ancient ay, saying, the land your feet have trodden shall be yours and your children's forever because you have faithfully followed the Lord your God. Caleb then said to Joshua: Give me this mountain for I am as strong today as I was fourty-five years ago when Moses made me this promise, and I shall be able to drive them (the giants) out, as the Lord said. **"And Joshua blessed him, and gave onto Caleb the son of Jephun'-neh Hebron for an inheritance. He-bron therefore became the inheritance of Caleb the son of Jephun'-neh** the Kenezite unto this day, because that he wholly followed the Lord God of Israel." *Joshua14:13-14*

The fact that giants lived on until the time of King David is obvious from the fact that the young David killed Goliath and later his family and friends continued fighting the Philistines, who were then led by Goliath's four brothers. **"And there was war again with the Phillstines; and Elhanan the son of Jair slew Lahmi the brother of Goliath the Gittite, whose spear staff was like a weaver's beam. And yet again there was war at Gath, where was a man of great stature, whose fingers and toes were four and twenty, six on each hand, and six on each foot: and he also was the son of the giant. But when he defiled Israel, Jonathan the son of Shimea David's brother slew him. These were born unto the giant in Gath; and they fell by the hand of David, and by the** measurements various cultures went by. The Prophet Amos however may have provided us with a small clue. **"Yet destroyed I the Amorite before them, whose height was like the height of the cedars, and he was strong as the oaks; Yet I destroyed his fruit from above, and his roots from beneath."** *Amos 2:9*

Joshua and the Children of Israel were not successful in completely exterminating the giants as God had instructed them to do. Although Joshua eliminated the descendants of the Anakim from the high country of Hebron, Debir, and Anab, several remained alive in Ashdod, Gaza, and Gath. **"And at that time came Joshua, and cut off the Anakims from the mountains, from Hebron, from Debir, from Anab, and from all the mountains of Judah, and from all of the mountains of Israel: Joshua destroyed them utterly with their cities. There were none of the Akims left in the land of the children of Israel: only in Gaza, in Gath, and in Ashdod, there remained."** *Joshua 11:21-22*

The faithful spy Caleb then traveled to Gilgal and spoke to Joshua in order to claim his inheritance which Moses had promised him forty-five years earlier for his faithful report of the Promised Land. Caleb said to Joshua: Remember what God said to Moses forty-five years ago in Kadesh-barnea, concerning the claim I made over the City of Hebron, for I am well able to take it. In the *New Testament* Jesus told us that as it was in the days of Noah, it would be again in the last days. If there were giants in the land in the beginning of the *Old Testament*, there will be giants in the earth again at the end of the *New Testament. The Septuagint* states: **"The Vision which**

Esaias (Isaiah) son of Amos saw against Babylon. Lift up a standard on the mountain of the plain, exalt the voice to them, beckon with the hand, open the gates, ye rulers. I give command, and I bring them: giants are coming to fulfil my wrath, rejoicing at the same time and insulting. A voice of many nations on the mountains, even like to that of many nations; a voice of kings and nations gathered together: the Lord of hosts has given command to a war-like nation, to come from a land afar off, from the utmost foundation of heaven; the Lord and his warriors are coming to destroy all the world." *Isaiah 13:1-5*

"But as the days of Noe (Noah) were so shall also the coming of the Son of man be. For as in the days that were before the flood they were eating and drinking, marrying and giving in marriage, until the day that Noe entered into the ark, And knew not until the flood came, and took them all away; so shall also the coming of the Son of man be." *Matthew 24:37-39*

Chapter 9

The Promised Seed

"But we speak the wisdom of God in a mystery, even the hidden wisdom, which God ordained before the world unto our glory. Which none of the princes of this world knew: for had they known it, they would not have crucified the Lord of glory." *I Corinthians 2:7-8*

Yes, the godhead had successfully hid their secret plan of redemption, and salvation from Satan, for if he had completely understood it he would have known the cross, and the resurrection of Christ would be the instruments of his ultimate defeat. Satan is a scripture lawyer, who, is a master of taking scriptures out of context, and turning them to say something God never intended. Satan, however could simply not comprehend the fact that, through a virgin, the victory he had earlier won over the First Adam (read *Romans* 5:14), would be lost to Emanuel, the Last Adam, who was God, in the flesh, with us. "Therefore the Lord himself shall give you a sign; Behold, a virgin shall conceive, and bear a son, and shall call his name Immanuel." *Isiah 7:14*

"But now is Christ risen from the dead, and become the first-fruits of them that sleep. For since by man came death, by man came also the resurrection of the dead. For as in Adam all die, even so in Christ shall all be made alive." *I Corinthians 15:22*

"And so it is written, the first man Adam was made a living soul; the last Adam was made a quickening (life giving) spirit." *I Corinthians 15:45*

"The first man is of the earth, earthly: the second man is the Lord from heaven." *I Corinthians 15:47*

"But when the fullness of the time was come, God sent forth his son, made of a woman, made under the law. To redeem them that were under the law, that we might receive the adoption of sons." *Galations 4:4-5*

After thousands of years, the Sign-Woman would finally deliver the Promised Seed for all to see, but before his birth only a hand full of people knew it was about to happen. The Scribes, Pharisees, Sadducees, and King Herod were all oblivious to the soon coming birth. The first to know of the birth were the Magi who were living far off in Babylon and quickly left, following the star, all the way to Bethlehem. Another person to know of the soon coming birth was an old man living in Jerusalem named Simeon. **"And, behold, there was a man in Jerusalem, whose name was Simeon; and the same man was just and devout, waiting for the consolation of Israel: and the Holy Ghost was upon him. And it was revealed unto him by the Holy Ghost, that he should not see death, before he had seen the Lord's Christ."** *Luke 2:25-26*

As Simeon was patiently awaiting the fulfillment of this promise, Satan, no doubt, was aware of something stirring in the heavenly angelic realm, but what did all this activity really mean? The Jews were looking for a Messiah that would throw off the yoke of Roman-bondage from the chosen-people, but how would he first appear? The Magi were looking for a king, a king which Herod could not tolerate. What was Satan looking for? An unmarried-virgin had never before given birth to a child. It is unlikely that Satan and his fallen angels were on the lookout for a virgin to conceive a son, in an obscure, far-off place like Nazareth. **"And in the sixth month the angel Gabriel was sent from God unto a city of Galilee, named Nazareth, To a virgin espoused to a man whose name was Joseph, of the house of David; and the virgin's name was Mary. And the angel came in unto her, and said, Hail, thou that are highly favoured, the Lord is with thee: blessed art thou among women. And when she saw him, she was troubled at his saying, and was troubled at his saying, and cast in her mind what manner of salutation this should be."** *Luke1:26-29*

Just imagine if you were Mary, an unmarried-virgin, and you were told by an angel you would soon become pregnant, something that had never happened in recorded history. This child was not only to be supernaturally conceived, but he was also to be a king, and sit on the throne of King David. Would you doubt the possibility of such a thing, or would you react with the same kind of faith Mary did? **"And, behold, thou shalt conceive in thy womb, and bring forth a son, and shalt call his name Jesus. He shall be great, and shall be called the Son of the Highest: and the Lord God shall give unto him the throne of his father David. And he shall** reign over the house of Jacob for ever; and of his kingdom there shall be no end. Then said Mary unto the angel, How shall this be, seeing I now not a man?" *Luke1:31-34*

The angel Gabriel was patient with Mary's question as to how this pregnancy was to be accomplished without having sex with a man. Mary's question did not show a hint of doubt, but only curiosity as to how such a thing was possible. You or I could be forgiven for asking the same legitimate question. **"And the angel answered and said unto her, The Holy Ghost shall come upon thee, and the power of the Highest shall over-shadow thee: therefore also that holy thing which shall be born of thee shall be called the Son of God. And, behold, thy cousin Elisabeth, she hath also conceived a son in her old age: and this is the sixth month with her, who was called barren. For with God nothing shall be impossible."** *Luke 1:35-37*

Did Mary fully realize she was about to be chosen to give birth to the long-awaited Messiah, the promised-seed, spoken of all the way back in the Garden of Eden? Whether she understood all the ramifications of Gabriel's words concerning herself, and her cousin Elisabeth is not clear. Mary however showed a tremendous amount of faith by consented to Gabriel's words, saying, let all these things happen to me. **"And Mary said, Behold the handmaiden of the Lord; be it unto me according to thy word. And the angel departed from her."** *Luke 1:38*

The supernatural impregnation of both Mary and Elisabeth at the same time, served to strengthen the faith of both women. After John the Baptist was born and grew to adulthood, all the promises made to Zacharias and Elisabeth by the angel Gabriel came true. **"And when Zacharias saw him, he was troubled, and fear fell upon him. But the angel said unto him, Fear not, Zacharias: for thy prayer is heard; and thy wife Elisabeth shall bear thee a son, and thou shalt call his name John. And thou shalt have joy and gladness; and many shall rejoice at his birth. For he shall be great in the sight of the Lord, and shall drink neither wine nor strong drink; and he shall be filled with the Holy Ghost, even from his mother's womb."** *Luke 1:12-15*

John's mission in life was to prepare the hearts of the people to receive their promised Messiah, by water baptism for the confession and remission of their sins. John began his ministry in the wilderness by saying he baptized with water, but the Christ would baptize the people with the Holy Ghost. "And there went out unto him all the land of Judea, and they of Jerusalem, and were all baptized of him in the river Jordan, concerning their sins. And John was clothed with camel's hair, and with a girdle of a skin about his loins; and he did eat locusts and wild honey; and preached, saying, There cometh one mightier than I after me, the latchet of whose shoes I am not worthy to stoop down and unloosen. I indeed have baptized you with water: but he shall baptize you with the Holy Ghost." *Mark 1:5-8*

"There was a man sent from God, whose name was John. The same came for a witness, to bear witness of the light, that all men through him might believe. He was not that Light, but was sent to bear witness of that light. That was the true Light, which lighteth every man that cometh into the world." *John 1:6-9*

"And as the people were in expectation, and all men mused in their hearts of John, whether he were the Christ, or not; John answered, saying unto them all, I indeed baptize you with water; but one mightier than I cometh, the latchet of whose shoes I am not worthy to unloose: he shall baptize you with the Holy Ghost and with fire: Whose fan is in his hand, and he will thoroughly purge his floor, and will gather the wheat into his garner; but the chaff he will burn with fire unquenchable." *Luke 3:15-17*

King Herod had known nothing of the birth of Christ until the Magi told him of the star that had led them from Babylon to Bethlehem. "Now when Jesus was born in Bethlehem of Judea in the days of Herod the king, behold, there came wise men from the east to Jerusalem, Saying, Where is he that is born King of the Jews? For we have seen his star in the east, and are come to worship him." *Matthew 2:1-2*

The Scribes, Pharisees, and High Priest knew nothing of the birth until Herod summoned them to inquire where the Christ would be born. Herod would never have thought an out of the way place such as Bethlehem, would be the birthplace of the promised Messiah, yet, this is what he was told: "And when he had gathered all the chief priests and scribes of the people together, he demanded of them where Christ should be born. And they said unto him, In Bethlehem of Judea: for thus it is written by the prophet (Micah 5:2), **And thou Bethlehem, in the land of Judea, art not the least among the princes of Judea: for out of thee shall come a Governor, that shall rule my people Israel."** *Matthew 2:4-6*

Although the scribes knew of the birthplace of Christ, neither they, nor Herod were expecting his arrival, even though it was spoken of many times in the *Old Testament*. Satan however was quite aware that his long awaited showdown with the promised-seed was at hand, and quickly set about to kill him at his birth. Because King Herod could not pinpoint the birth of the child, he issued a decree to kill all the children in Bethlehem, two years old and under. **"Then Herod, when he saw that he was mocked of the wise men, was exceeding wroth, and sent forth, and slew all the children that were in Bethlehem, and in all the coasts thereof, from two years old and under, according to the time which he had diligently inquired of the wise men. Then was fulfilled that which was spoken by Jeremy the prophet** (Jeremiah 31:15), **saying, In Rama was there a voice heard, lamentation, and weeping, and great mourning, Rachel weeping for her children, and would not be comforted, because they are not."** *Matthew 16:18*

Joseph and Mary had been warned by an angel that Herod would try to kill the child, thus they quickly migrated to Egypt where they remained until Herod's death. Upon returning to Judea, Joseph and Mary learned that Herod's son Chelaus was setting on his father's throne, thus they quickly traveled north, all the way to Galilee, where they settled down in the tiny town of Nazareth, thus Jesus would be called a Nazarene: **"And he came and dwelt in a city called Nazareth: that it might be fulfilled which was spoken by the prophets, He shall be called a Nazarene."** *Matthew 2:23*

During their stay in Nazareth a decree from Cesar Augustus, was sent throughout all the Roman-world, announcing a tax on all families, to be paid in their perspective home-towns. Because Joseph was of the house and linage of King David, he would have to travel all the way to Bethlehem to pay these taxes. **"And so it was, that, while they were there** (in Bethlehem), **the days were accomplished that she should be delivered. And she brought forth her firstborn son, and wrapped him in swaddling clothes, and laid him in a manger; because there was no room in the inn."** *Luke 2:6-7*

According to the Law of Moses, eight days after the birth of every Male child there was to be a circumcision, and an offering of two turtledoves, or pigeons. To accomplish this Joseph and Mary had to hurry off to Jerusalem to fulfill the law, and present Jesus to the Lord. **"And when they had performed all things according to the law of the Lord, they returned into Galilee, to their own city Nazareth. And the child grew, and waxed strong in spirit, filled with wisdom: and the grace of God was upon him."** *Luke 2:39-40*

Every year Joseph and Mary traveled with Jesus back down to Jerusalem to observe the feast of Passover. At age twelve, Jesus was separated from his family for three days, and later was found in the Temple, debating with the doctors of the Law. **"And he said unto them, how is it that ye sought me? wist ye not that I must be about my Father's business. And they understood not the saying which he spake unto them. And he went down with them, and came to Nazareth, and was subject unto them: but his mother kept all these sayings in her heart. And Jesus increased in wisdom and stature, and in favour with God and man."** *Luke 2:49-52*

After thirty years the day finally came for Jesus to begin his earthly ministry, thus he traveled to Jerusalem to be baptized by John the Baptist in the Jordan. **"Then cometh Jesus from Galilee to Jordan unto John, to be baptized of him. But John forbad him, saying, I have need to be baptized of thee, and comest thou to me? And Jesus answering said unto him, Suffer it to be so now: for thus it becometh us to fulfil all righteousness. Then he suffered him. And Jesus, when he was bsptized, went up straightway out of the water: and, lo, the heavens were opened unto him, and he saw the Spirit of God descending like a dove, and lighting upon him: And lo a voice from heaven saying, This is my beloved Son, in whom I am well pleased."** *Matthew 4:13-17*

There are about three hundred prophecies in the *Old Testament* about Jesus, thus, he came to earth in the flesh to fulfill all of them. There are about six hundred and fifty regulations in the Law of Moses, and Jesus never broke one of them, thus he was the only flesh and blood man to be without sin. If Satan could tempt Jesus to use his power and authority as the Son of God, apart from his Father's will, Satan could appear before the Throne of God and accuse Jesus of being rebellious to God's will. Jesus had all power in heaven and earth and had a freewill to obey God, or not, just as Adam and Eve had in the Garden of Eden. Satan's first temptation came just after Jesus was baptized by John the Baptist, and was led into the wilderness to be tempted for forty days. **"And Jesus being full of the Holy Ghost returned from Jordan, and was led by the Spirit into the wilderness, Being forty days tempted of the devil. And in those days did eat nothing: and when they were ended, he afterward hungered. And the devil said unto him, If thou be the Son of God, command this stone that it be made bread. And Jesus answered him, saying, It is written, That man shall not live by bread alone, but by every word of God."** *Luke 4:1-4*

"And when the tempter came to him, he said, if thou be the Son of God, command that these stones be made bread. But he (Jesus) answered and said, It is written, Man shall not live by bread alone, but by every word that proceedeth out of the mouth of God." *Matthew 4:3-4*

Even after forty days of fasting, Jesus resisted Satan's first temptation to use his power to make bread from the stones, simply to provide for his physical needs. Satan tempted Jesus a second time to misuse his power by taking him to the top of the temple, saying: throw yourself down to prove you truly are Son of God. Jesus knew that if he had accidentally fallen from the pinnacle of the temple, his guardian angels would have protected him. However, to intentionally throw yourself from the pinnacle of the temple was to tempt God. **"Then the devil taketh him up into the holy city, and setteth him on a pinnacle of the temple, And said unto him, If thou be the Son of God, cast thyself down: for it is written, He shall give his angels charge concerning thee: and in their hands they shall bear thee up, lest at any time thou dash thy foot against a stone. And Jesus said unto him, It is written again, Thou shall not tempt the Lord thy God."** *Matthew 4:5-7*

"And he brought him to Jerusalem, and set him on a pinnacle of the temple, and said to him, If thou be the Son of God, cast thyself down from hence: For it is written, He shall give his angels charge over thee, to keep thee: And in their hands they shall bear thee up, lest at any time thou dash thy foot against a stone. And Jesus answering said unto him, It is said, Thou shalt not tempt the Lord thy God." *Luke 4:9-12*

Jesus resisted Satan's second temptation to use his power just to prove he was the true Son of God. Jesus was not going to test God's grace by doing something stupid like jumping off the top of the Temple. Satan's third temptation came when he took Jesus up into a high mountain and showed him all the glory of all the kingdoms of the world. Satan claimed he had authority over all these kingdoms and could give that power and authority to anyone he chose. **"And the devil, taking him up into a high mountain, showed unto him all the kingdoms of the world in a moment of time. And the devil said unto him, All this power will I give thee, and the glory of them: for that is delivered to me; and to whomsoever I will give it. If thou therefore wilt worship me, all shall be thine. And Jesus answered and said unto him, Get thee behind me, Satan: for it is written, Thou shalt worship the Lord thy God, and him only shalt thou serve."** *Luke 4:5-8*

"Again, the devil taketh him up into an exceeding high mountain, and showeth him all the kingdoms of the world, and the glory of them; And sayeth unto him, All these things will I give thee, if thou wilt fall down and worship me. Then Jesus said unto him, Get thee hence, Satan: for it is written, Thou shalt worship the Lord thy God, and him only shalt thou serve." *Matthew 4:8-10*

Jesus remembered all the glory he had had with God the Father long before the world ever existed, thus Satan's last temptation, meant little to him. The Promised Seed had weathered the best temptation Satan could throw at him, and, by quoting Gods Word, had defeated Satan at his own game. **"And now, o Father, glorify thou me with thine own self with the glory which I had with thee before the world was."** *John 17: 5*

Yes, Satan had tried every trick on Jesus to cause him to sin against his Father's Word, yet, Jesus remained without sin. Where the First Adam had failed by yielding to Satan's temptations, even before he was crucified, the Last Adam, Jesus, triumphed over Satan. Jesus crushed Satan's authority over mankind, and showed him up as the thief and lire he always was. **"And having spoiled principalities and powers, he made a show of them openly, triumphing over them in it."** *Colossians 2:15*

Chapter 10

The Pentecostal Church

From all across the world at this same time each year, Jews began trickling into Jerusalem to celebrate a series of feasts known as the "Four Spring Feasts," which, all together would last about sixty days. All Jews understood the meaning of Passover, and the story of their deliverance out of Egypt. The second of these four feasts happened one day after Passover and was known as Unleavened Bread. The third of these four feasts happened two days after Unleavened Bread, and was called First Fruits, but its meaning was much more obscure, and mysterious to the Jews than Passover, or Unleavened Bread. Most Jews understood that First Fruits had something to do with planting their crops of grain, but they were not sure exactly what it was all about. Each year, after the Jew's grain had been sowed in their fields, a priest would inspect the fields each morning, watching for the first emerging sprouts. Finally, one morning, there it was, the first sprout to break ground. The priest slowly, and carefully lifted the sprout out of the ground and carried it back to the Temple. There, the priest held the sprout up before the alter and began waving it back and forth before God. The priests knew how to perform the ritual of First Fruits, but they had no real idea of what its significance was, or what it was really was all about. Most Jews left Jerusalem after celebrating First Fruits, but some would stay in town for the additional fifty days, until the Feast of Pentecost. Almost none of the Jews, including the doctors of the Law, had any real idea of the true spiritual significance of Pentecost, only that it happened fifty days after First Fruits. In hindsight, after reading our *New Testament*, we can now better understand the significance of these four feasts. Jesus was born on September 11th, (9-11), during the Fall-Feast of Trumpets, which is also known as Rosh HaShanah, or Yom Teruah. Jesus was the perfect sacrificial lamb, crucified on Passover, also known as Pesach. Jesus was buried, and descended into Abraham's Bosom, in the underworld on the first day of the Feast of Unleavened Bread, or Hag HaMatzah. Jesus was raised from the dead on the morning of First Fruits, or HaBikkurim. The outpouring of the

Holy Spirit was poured out on the Church after Jesus returned to Heaven, during the Feast of Weeks, or Pentecost, which is also known as Shavuot. I personally believe Jesus will return to this earth again at sunset, during the Feast of Trumpets, at the sounding of the seventh, or last trumpet. Again, in hindsight, we can now better understand the words of Jesus when he said: **"Think not that I am come to destroy the law, or the prophets: I am not come to destroy, but to fulfill. For verily I say unto you, Till heaven and earth, pass, one jot or one tittle shall in no wise pass from the law, till all be fulfilled."** *Matthew 5:17-18*

The Church first officially began fifty days after the Resurrection of Christ, and ten days after his Ascension, on the Day of Pentecost, in the late spring of 30 A.D.. For the next five weeks Jesus would appear to many of his disciples and even ate food with them. On the fortieth day after his resurrection, Jesus instructed his disciples to wait in Jerusalem until they would receive the Holy Spirit, and power. Jesus then ascended into heaven in the presence of all those gathered together on the top of the Mount of Olives. The one thing all the disciples had in common was their belief that Jesus was the long-awaited Messiah of Israel, their Christ. The word Messiah in the Hebrew, and the word Christ in the Greek, both mean the Anointed One. The word Pentecost means fifty, thus it was God's plan that fifty days after Passover, on the Day of Pentecost, his Church would be endued with power. It was Jesus' plan that like him, all of his disciples should become Anointed Ones, thus he commanded them, before venturing outside of Jerusalem to preach, that they should all wait for the baptism of the Holy Spirit. **"And being assembled together with them, commanded them that they should not depart from Jerusalem, but wait for the promise of the Father, which, saith he, Ye have heard of me. For John truly baptized with water; but ye shall be baptized with the Holy Ghost not many days hence."** *Acts 1:4-5*

As Jesus stood on the Mount of Olives, just as he was about to ascend back to heaven, he again reminded his disciples not to leave Jerusalem until they were given the power to be witness of him, not only there in Jerusalem, but also throughout the whole world.

"But ye shall receive power, after that the Holy Ghost is come upon you: and ye shall be witnesses unto me both in Jerusalem, and in all Judea, and in Samaria, and unto the uttermost part of the earth." *Acts 1:8*

The disciples headed Jesus' warning and one hundred and twenty of them were gathered in one place, praying and waiting on God. Suddenly, they heard a strange sound like a rushing mighty wind, followed by small flames of fire, falling and resting upon the heads of all assembled there. **"And when the day of Pentecost was fully come, they were all with one accord in one place. And suddenly there came a sound from heaven as of a rushing mighty wind, and it filled all the house where they were sitting. And there appeared unto them cloven tongues like as of fire, and it sat upon each of them. And they were all filled with the Holy Ghost, and began to speak with other tongues, as the Spirit gave them utterance."** *Acts 2:1-4*

This experience was not only limited to those hundred and twenty Jews speaking in tongues inside the room, but spilled out into the streets for all to hear and see. There were three feast days each year, when all Jewish males were compelled to attend in Jerusalem, Passover, Pentecost, and Tabernacles. Because of this there were thousands of Jews in Jerusalem that day, visiting from all around the Middle-East, and the world, celebrating Pentecost. All of these visitors could both see, and hear what was happening, but they had no rational expiation as to what it all meant. The hundred and twenty were speaking in various languages they themselves did not know, but the visiting Jews from around the world, could understand their words. **"And there were dwelling at Jerusalem Jews, devout men, out of every nation under heaven. Now when this was noised abroad, the multitude came together, and were confounded, because that every man heard them speak in his own language. And they were all amazed and marveled, saying one to another, Behold, are not all these which speak Galileans? And now hear we every man in our own tongue, wherein we were born."** *Acts 2:5-8*

What the visitors were hearing was a group of uneducated Galileans speaking in perfect dialects, the native languages of devout-Jews from around the world. Most of these Galileans probably understood Hebrew, Greek, and Aramaic, but they certainly did not know Latin, Syriac, Arabic, Armenian, or any other languages. The common theme they all spoke was to praise, and magnify God for all his wonderful works. How could uneducated Galileans, recount all the wonderful works of God, in so many different languages they had never learned? It was all quite confusing as some speculated they were all simply drunk. **"And they were all amazed, and** were in doubt, saying one to another, What meaneth this? Others mocking said, These men are full of new wine. But Peter, standing up with the eleven, lifted up his voice, and said unto them, Ye men of Judea, and all ye that dwell at Jerusalem, be this known unto you, and hearken to my words. For these are not drunken as ye suppose, seeing it is but the third hour of the day. But this is that which was spoken by the prophet Joel." *Acts 2:12-16*

"And it shall come to pass afterwards, that I will pour out my spirit upon all flesh; and your sons and daughters shall prophecy, your old men shall dream dreams, your young men shall see visions: And also upon the servants and upon the handmaids in those days will I pour out my spirit." *Joel 2:28-29*

Peter, after quoting the prophet Joel, explained to all the people that this prophecy had just been fulfilled right before their eyes. Speaking of the resurrection of Christ, Peter explained to all the people that after Jesus was seated at the right hand of God the Father, he sent down to earth the Holy Spirit to empower, and embolden his disciples. **"This Jesus hath God raised up, wherefore we all are witnesses. Therefore being by the right hand of God exalted, and having received of the Father the promise of the Holy Ghost, he hath shed forth this, which ye now see and hear."** *Acts 2:32-33*

Peter, no doubt, was thinking back to the words Jesus spoke during the Last Supper. There, Jesus told his disciples it was time for him to leave them, but after he was gone, the Father would send them the Comforter to help, and empower them to do even greater works than he had done. This is what Jesus meant when he said it is better for you that I go away, for if I don't go to heaven, the Holy Spirit will not come to earth. **"These things have I spoken unto you, being yet present with you. But the Comforter, which is the Holy Ghost, whom the Father will send in my name, he shall teach you all things, and bring all things to your remembrance, whatsoever I have said unto you."** *John 14:25-26*

"But when the Comforter is come, whom I will send unto you from the Father, even the Spirit of truth, which proceedeth from the Father, he shall testify of me," *John 15:26*

"Nevertheless I tell you the truth, It is expedient for you that I go

away: for if I go not away, the Comforter will not come unto you; but if I depart, I will send him unto you. And when he is come, he will reprove the world of sin, and of righteousness, and of judgment." *John 16:7-8*

"Howbeit when he, the Spirit of truth, is come, he will guide you into all truth: for he shall not speak of himself; but whatsoever he shall hear, that shall he speak: and he will show you things to come. He shall glorify me: for he shall receive of mine, and shall show it unto you." *John 16:13-14*

On the day of Pentecost, the Church grew from about one hundred and twenty Jews, to several thousand. All the visiting Jews soon migrated back to their home-towns and quickly related the strange events that had just happened in Jerusalem to their friends and family. Soon, small groups of Jewish-Christians began meeting in Synagogues throughout Palestine, the Middle-East, and Turkey. The Jewish-Church in Jerusalem however remained the center of Messianic-Jewish life for the first fifty years of the first century Church. This all began to slowly change as the Apostle Paul was called and gifted to reach out to these same small Messianic groups of Jews throughout the Middle East. Paul was born in Tarsus the capital city of Cilicia, located in Asia Minor, where the predominate pagan god worshiped was the sun-god Mithras. The god Mithra spring from the old Babylonian religion known as Zoroastrianism, whose supreme deity was Ahura Mazda. There were many Mithraic Temples throughout the Middle-east with priests who were called Fathers, and priestesses who were called Holy-Mothers, or Madonna's. As a young boy, Paul had been taught that Mithra was born in a cave, to a virgin mother on December 25th, and received the adoration of shepherds soon after his birth. Mithra had been put to death at the time of the year we call Easter, then, after three days, he was raised from the dead. Mithraists also believed in an eternal life in heaven, and in an eternal judgement, and torture for the wicked after death. Paul had been born into a Roman Mithraic family who had converted to Judaism. As Greek-speaking Jews, they gave their son the Greek name of Paulos, but in Hebrew he was called Saul. Wherever Saul, later to be called Paul, traveled to preach, he would first began preaching in these synagogues, and would from there, reach out to the pagan Gentiles. Because he had been raised as a child in a city filled with sun worshippers, Paul had a special revelation that better equipped him to understand the love God had for the entire world, Jews and pagan Gentiles alike. Paul also had a special revelation of the body of

Christ, and the various gifts of the Holy Spirit to equip Christ's body to function as the Church. Wherever Paul preached his emphases was always on the fact that the Church was the literal body of Christ on earth. Jesus was the greatest apostle, prophet, evangelist, pastor, and teacher that ever walked the earth. When Jesus ascended to heaven to sit at the right-hand of God the Father, the Holy Spirit descended back to earth with various ministry, and personal gifts to act as Christ's body on earth. **"But unto every one of us is given grace according to the measure of the gift of Christ. Wherefore he saith, When he ascended up on high, he led captivity captive, and gave gifts unto men."** *Ephesians 4:7-8*

These gifts are not meant for our own personal edification, but were given to each of us for the edification and building up of the whole body of Christ. These gifts do not operate in our own lives as we would choose, but operate how, and when the Holy Spirit chooses. We are to earnestly desire the functioning of these gifts in our own personal lives in order to be a blessing to the Church as a whole. Generally speaking, we can categories these various gifts, first as ministry gifts, and second as personal gifts of Grace. The first of these two categories are the five-fold ministry gifts which are given to certain men and women to be a blessing to the whole Church. **"And he gave some, apostles; and some, prophets; and some, evangelists; and some; and some, pastors and teachers; For the perfecting of the saints, for the work of the ministry, for the edifying of the body of Christ: Till we all come in the unity of the faith, and of the knowledge of the Son of God, unto a perfect man, unto the measure of the stature of the fullness of Christ."** *Ephesians 4:11-13*

Although this author has functioned in the ministry office of a pastor, my primary ministry gift is that of a teacher. The primary work of the apostles, prophets, evangelists, pastors, and teachers is to equip the Church to do the work of the ministry. The success of the first-century church lay in the fact that they understood, and practiced body-ministry. The five-fold ministers recognized the gifts within various believers and moved to place each of them within their different callings, and unique sphere of influence. In this way it was not just a few professional preachers doing the work of the ministry, but the whole church stopped being spectators, thus they changed the world. Most Christians today are lounging, and being entertained in what I call Christian country clubs, not knowing they should be reporting to the front lines of the battlefield. In the case of the five-fold ministry gifts, it is the person himself which must first understand, and then prepare before he can be given as a gift to the Body of Christ. Few Christians are called to a five-fold ministry office, but all Christians are given a mission, and personal grace gifts to fulfill their mission, and individual callings. If our churches today operated on that same principal, we would have the same results the first-century church had in pushing back the darkness of the pagan world. Unfortunately almost all of our churches today believe these gifts were only for the early church and today have disappeared. This sad fact is not only true of most denominational churches, but it is also true of some of our so-called charismatic churches, who say they believe in the gifts, but never allow them to be manifest. In the early church, soon after someone was born again they were sent to a spiritual boot camp and taught all the strategies and tricks of the enemy. There they learned that the gifts of the Holy Spirit were the weapons of their warfare, the guns, knives, swords, and spears, to be used against Satan and all his demonic hosts. They were not expected to enter the battle until they understood how to use these weapons, and function within the framework of the gifts of the Spirit. Like Jesus, they were then sent out to destroy all the works of the devil. **"Now there are diversities of gifts** (chrisma), **but the same Spirit. And there are differences of administrations, but the same Lord. And there are diversities of operations, but it is the same God which worketh all in all. But the manifestation of the Spirit is given to every man to profit withal. For to one is given by the Spirit the word of wisdom; to another the word of knowledge; by the same Spirit.; To another faith by the same Spirit; to another the gifts of healing by the same Spirit; To another the working of miracles; to another prophecy; to another discerning of spirits; to another divers kinds of tongues; to another the interpretation of tongues."** *I Corinthians 12:4-10*

These nine manifestations of the Holy Spirit are not earned, but rather are gifts given by grace to Christians for the benefit of the whole body of Christ. Unlike the nine fruit of the Spirit, these nine supernatural gifts of the Spirit are momentary manifestations, and are not dependent on the character, or maturity of the believer. The Corinthian Church was a classic example of how the gifts of the Spirit often worked in the lives of immature, and often immoral Christians. A few years ago there was a very famous evangelist who operated in several gifts of the Spirit, but unknown to most people, he was an alcoholic. Most people thought he had to have lived a very sanctified, and holy life for all these gifts to operate through him, but he died from alcoholism. Unlike the nine fruit of the Spirit, the nine super-natural gifts of the Spirit manifest in a moment of time, while the fruit of the Spirit requires repentance and attention to God's word over time. Like any fruit tree, the fruit first appears as a blossom, but then it takes time and sometimes cultivation for it to grow to the point you can recognize which fruit it is. All of the gifts of the Spirit, whether personal grace gifts, or minis-try gifts, are given without repentance on God's part. This means despite the maturity, character, or moral condition of the Christian, God never takes back his gifts which were given for the edification of the Body of Christ, and to glorify God. **"As every man hath received the gift, even so minister the same one to another, as good Stewarts of the manifold** (many sided) **grace of God. If any man speak, let him speak as the oracles of God; if any man minister, let him do it as of the ability which God giveth: that God in all things may be glorified through Jesus Christ, to whom be praise and dominion for ever and ever Amen."** *I Peter 4:10-11*

The apostle Paul, when writing to the Corinthians, reminded them that every part of a human body is totally dependent on all the other parts, thus none are unimportant. **"For the body is not one member, but many. If the foot shall say, Because I am not the hand, I am not of the body; is it therefore not of the body? If the whole body were an eye, where were the hearing? If the whole were hearing, where were smelling? But now hath God set the members every one of them in the body, as it hath pleased him. And if they were all one member, where were the body. But now are they many members, yet but one body."** *I Corinthians 12:14-20*

Of all the Gentile churches the Apostle Paul established, none were more gifted than the Corinthians, yet, they were babies when it came to understanding, and using their gifts. Yes, the Corinthian were the most gift-ed, but they were also the most selfish and contentious with each other, because they were not properly discerning the body of Christ. They didn't understand that they needed each other, and they should treat each other as a literal member of Christ's own body. The Corinthian Christians had been raised in a city where the pagan Temple of Aphrodite ruled over its leaders, and provided temple prostitutes, both male, and female, to its citizens. The Corinthians had a perverted concept of both sex, and the family, thus they were a very immoral people. The apostle Paul had to teach them they should not join the body of Christ, with the body of a prostitute.

"Now ye are the body of Christ, and members in particular. And God hath set some in the church, first apostles, secondarily prophets, thirdly teachers, after that miracles, then gifts of healings, helps, governments, diversities of tongues. Are all apostles? Are all prophets? Are all teachers? Are all workers of miracles? Have all the gifts of healing? Do all speak with tongues? Do all interpret?" *I Corinthians 12:27-30*

In all there are nine personal grace gifts namely: the Word of Wisdom; the Word of knowledge; Faith; Gifts of healing; the Working of miracles; Prophecy; the Discerning of spirits; Divers kinds of tongues; Interpretation of tongues. The first seven of these gifts can be seen manifested in the Old Testament, but tongues, and interpretation of tongues were added in the Church-age. In order to bring clarity, theologians have often broken these nine gifts into three sub-groups namely: Gifts of Revelation; Gifts of Power; and Gifts of Inspiration. The three gifts of revelation are the word of wisdom, the word of knowledge, and the discerning of spirits. The three gifts of power are faith, gifts of working miracles, and gifts of healing. The three gifts of inspiration are prophecy, different kinds, or diversities of tongues, and the interpretation of tongues. All manifestations of these nine gifts are given by the Holy Spirit, manifesting himself in nine distinctive ways. All of these personal grace gifts function differently in each individual, but they are all given and divided to every individual in the Church, as the Holy Spirit wills. The two personal grace gifts of tongues, and interpretation of tongues are the two supernatural manifestations which characterizes the modern-day Pentecostal Church. Speaking with other tongues is the initial sign of the last-days outpouring of the Holy Spirit, spoken of by the prophet Joel. This was true on the Day of Pentecost, and it is still true today. The greatest, and most powerful manifestation of the Holy Spirit in a Christian's life is the Fruit of the Spirit that begins to form and grow as each area of a believers life is yielded to the authority of God's Word. **"But the fruit of the Spirit is love, joy, peace, longsuffering, gentleness, goodness, faith, meekness, temperance: against such there is no law."** *Galations 5:22-23*

The gifts of the Spirit served as powerful signs during the first-century Church, but it was the fruit of the Spirit in the lives of individual believers that most influenced the world. The First-Century Church manifested the fruit of the Spirit to such a degree, the Gentile world was astonished at the love they had for each other. Nowhere was this more true than in the city of Ephesus where the culture and economy of the city was completely dominated by the great pagan Temple of Diana. According to Greek mythology, Osiris fell madly in love with Apollo's sister Artemis, or Diana. Apollo was opposed to this union, thus, he tricked his sister Diana, into shooting an arrow into Osiris' head. When she saw how she had been tricked, Diana hid the dead body of Osiris among the stars and transformed him into the constellation Orion. Thereafter Orion was considered to be the soul of Osiris. Like the Corinthians, the Ephesians had both male, and female temple prostitutes, and their culture was completely dominated by the goddess Diana (read *Acts* 19:23-41), and steeped in idolatry, fornication, and immorality. After the Day of Pentecost, the Apostles were empowered to take the gospel to the whole world, but like many of us, were reluctant to move outside of their comfort zones. When the twelve apostles finally did leave Jerusalem and ventured out into all the gentile world to preach the gospel as Jesus had commissioned them to do, they ran headlong into four thousand years of Pagan traditions. At first the pagan world looked on the Christian-Gospel as a great heresy, especially in such cities as Rome, Ephesus, and Corinth, where great temples had been built to the pagan gods, and goddesses. As the first century gentile church grew it began to break up the political, intellectual, economic, and religious stranglehold these pagan temples had over all of these cities. The Apostle Paul warned the Corinthians that their temple sacrifices were, in fact, sacrifices to devils. **"But I say, that the things which the Gentiles sacrifice, they sacrifice to devils, and not to God: and I would not that ye should have fellowship with devils."** *I Corinthians 10:20*

There were secret societies attached to all of these pagan temples which controlled the politics, and economy of each of these cities. For example, in the city of Rome, an arcane group known as the Augurs (see Wikipedia), or bird watchers, ruled over its political affaires from behind the scenes. They were a group of temple-priests who practiced augury, which means they divined, and interpreted the will of the gods by watching the flight of birds. *Bible* scholar, and author Tom Horn, in his book *Apollyon Rising* states: **"The term 'inaugurate' is from the Latin *inauguratio* and refers to the archaic ceremony by which the Roman augurs (soothsayers) approved a king or ruler (or other action) through omens as being 'sanctioned by the gods.' As with Bush, the ancient 'inauguration' of the leader occurred after the priestly blessing and magical words were uttered, which assured the congregation and heads of state that the course of action was endorsed** by the gods. **The omens that the augurs used in determining the will of the gods included, among other things, thunder and lightning, as reflected in Bush's 'angel in the whirlwind' statements."** Another clear example of a pagan temple dominating a city is recorded in the Book of Revelation, when the last living apostle, the Apostle John is instructed by Christ to write letters to seven churches. In the city of Pergamum, Pergamon, or Pergamos, a large temple was built with a throne and alter inside, dedicated to Zeus. This throne, or seat, was over forty-foot high and surrounded with solid gold statues of all the Greek-gods. **"And to the angel of the church in Pergamos write; These things sayest he which hath the sharp sword with two edges. I know thy works and where thou dwellest, even where Satan's seat is: and thou holdest fast my name, and hast not denied my faith, even in the days wherein Antipas was my faithful martyr, who was slain among you, where Satan dwelleth."** *Revelation 2:12-13*

What little we know of Antipas comes from the traditions of the Eastern Orthodox Church which said that he had been ordained Bishop of Pergamos by the Apostle John. At the base of Pergamum's hill, there was large shrines erected to the Pagan God Asclepius, one of Apollo's sons. Because Asclepius supposedly had the power to raise people from the dead, Hades complained to Zeus, who killed him with one of hid thunderbolts. When Apollo complained to Zeus, that his son had done nothing worthy of death, Zeus repented and restored Asclepius back to life. From that time forward, Asclepius was worshiped as the "Savior God" of healing, who had the power to heal the sick, and raise the dead back to life. Asclepius was symbolized by a serpent winding about a pole, and was called the "Great Physician." Because Antipas was known to have cast out demons from people at the Shrine of Asclepius, he was later martyred on the Alter of Zeus by being roasted alive inside a copper bull, in 92 A.D, by the Roman Emperor Domitian. Antipas was just one of thousands of martyrs who paid the ultimate price for their resistance to the gentile pagan world. Jesus said that the Gates of Hell would not prevail against his church, thus, slowly but surley the church began to dismantle the pagan stranglehold it had had over the gentile world. In fact, in many places where the Pagans had earlier persecuted the Church, the church eventually turned the tables, and began to persecute the pagans. One of the greatest experts, and philosopher on Freemasonry, 33rd-Degree, Manly P. Hall, in his book The Secret Destany of America states: **"The rise of the Christian church broke up the intellectu-**

al pattern of the classical pagan world. By persecution of this pattern's ideologies it drove the secret societies into greater secrecy; the pagan intellectuals then refashoned their original ideas in a garment of Christian phraseology, but bestowed the keys of the symbolism only upon those duly initiated and bound to secrecy by their vows."

Chapter 11

Seven Feasts for Israel

"Speak unto the children of Israel, saying, The fifteenth day of this seventh month shall be the feast of tabernacles for seven days unto the Lord. On the first day shall be an holy convocation: ye shall do no servile work therein. Seven days ye shall offer an offering made by fire unto the Lord: it is a solemn assembly; and ye shall do no servile work therein." *Leviticus* 23:34-36

Recently, in America, there has been a reawakening among the Church concerning the seven ancient "Feasts of the Lord." All seven of these feasts will be celebrated each year during the thousand-year reign of Christ on earth known as the Millennium. God first revealed these feasts to Moses on Mount Saini, which he later recorded in the *Book of Leviticus*, which states: **"These are the feasts of the Lord, even holy convocations, which you shall proclaim in their seasons."** *Leviticus 23:2*

The *Septuagint* states: **"Speak to the children of Israel, and thou shalt say unto them, the feasts of the Lord which you shall call holy assemblies, these are my feasts."** *Leviticus 23:2*

The Hebrew word for feasts here is "mo'edim," which simply means a scheduled appointment, or appointed time. The Gentile Church has difficulty counting time in the same way the Jews do. We Gentiles, use the Gregorian calendar, created by Pope Gregory XIII, in 1582. The Gregorian calendar is basically the same as the Julian calendar except it drops three leap years every four centuries. Using the Gregorian calendar, we consider our days to begin and end at midnight. However the Jewish day begins and ends at the evening twilight, which technically, is the appearance of the first star in the evening. The Gregorian calendar is a "solar calendar," which means it is tied to the earth's revolving around the sun. It takes approximately 365.1/4 days for the earth to revolve entirely around the sun, thus every four years we have an extra day on our hands to deal with. This is why every four years we have a leap year of 366 days to make our calendar year accurate. The reason we Gentiles have a hard time with the Jewish calendar is because it is based on the "lunar calendar," which is based on the revolution of the moon around the earth. It takes approximately 29.1/2 days for the moon to make a complete rotation around the earth. Twelve of these lunar months adds up to about 354 days in a lunar year, which is 11.1/4 days shorter than a solar year. This difference requires the Jews to make a leap year adjustment to their calendar which consists of adding an extra month to their colander every third year, which is called the intercalary month. This intercalary month is 29 days long and keeps the Jewish lunar calendar accurate concerning the feast days, and the Sabbath days. If you have ever visited Jerusalem, you know everything shuts down for the weekly Sabbath on Friday evening. Businesses do not open up again until Saturday evening, at the appearance of the first star. The Jewish method of keeping time was also true in determining the beginning and ending of the Feast days. There were three Spring Feasts, one early summer feast, and three Fall Feasts, all of which were meant to point to some aspect of the life and ministry of our Lord Jesus Christ. There were three times each year, known as the "Pilgrimage Feasts", in which all Jewish males were required to make an appearance in Jerusalem to celebrate three of the seven feasts. **"Three times thou shalt keep a feast unto me in the year. Thou shalt keep the feast of unleavened bread: thou shalt eat unleavened bread seven days, as I commanded thee, in the time appointed of the month of Abib; for in it thou camest out from Egypt: and none shall appear before me empty. And the feast of harvest, the firstfruits of thy labors, which thou hast sown in the fields: and the feast of ingathering, which is in the end of the year, when thou hast gathered in thy labors out of the field. Three times in the year all thy males shall appear before the Lord God."** *Exodus 23:14-17*

"Three times in a year shall all thy males appear before the Lord thy God in the place which he shall choose; in the feast of unleavened bread, and in the feast of weeks (Pentecost), and in the feast of tabernacles: and they shall not appear before the Lord empty: Every man shall give as he is able, according to the blessing of the Lord thy God which he hath given thee." *Deuteronomy 16:16-17*

God commanded all Jewish males to appear before him in Jerusalem three times each year with their appropriate offerings in hand. Although there were seven different feasts, they were celebrated in what were called the "three feast seasons." The Feast of Passover was the first of the three feast seasons which included the Feasts of Passover, Unleavened Bread, and First Fruits. The second feast season included only Pentecost, which was a feast season unto itself. The third feast season was the Feast of Tabernacles, which included the Feasts of Trumpets, Atonement, and Tabernacles. These three feast seasons, with their various harvest offerings were directly tied to the different rainy seasons in Palestine. Each year the agricultural season began with the fall rainy season which happened in October and November, which softened the ground for plowing. This allowed both barley and wheat to be sown in the ground in November and December. The spring rainy season falls in March and April which allows the barley to be harvested. This also allows for the wheat to be harvest which happens in May and June. The grape harvest came soon after in the months of June and July. In July and August came the olive harvest, followed by the harvest of the dates and figs, which closed out the growing season. The dry summer season came during the Jewish months of Tammuz, Ab, and Elul, which lasts from June through September. This is followed by the winter rainy season which came again in December and January which allowed the almond trees to be harvested in January and February, and the citrus trees to be harvested in February and March.

The seven feasts were intended to serve as visual aids for the Jewish people so that they might better understand God's plan of redemption, and the ministry of their coming Messiah.

If you read the *Book of Acts*, you will find the Apostle Paul always personally observed the feast days, but he did not teach the Gentile Church to do the same. This is definitely why the Gentile Church has such little understanding of the various feasts, and their relationship to the fulfilment of *Bible* prophecy. After the martyrdom of the Apostles by the hands of the Pagans, the first century church began to slowly forget God's purposes in giving these seven feasts. By the time of the second century church, their meanings and practices had completely been lost by the Gentile Church. The Jews however did not forget the feasts, but they celebrated and observed them in so many different ways, according to their own man-made traditions, that, in time, they also lost the true meanings of most of the feasts, with the exception of Passover. On the rare occasion when the Apostle Paul did teach the Gentile Church about the different fests, he told them they were a shadow, or types, or rehearsal of things to come. But, because the Judaizes from Jerusalem were constantly trying to draw the Gentile Church back under the Mosaic laws, Paul warned the Church not to be caught in their trap. **"Let no man therefore judge you in meat, or in drink, in respect of an holyday, or of the new moon, or of the sabbath days: Which are a shadow of things to come."** *Colossians 3:16-17*

"For there are many unruly and vain talkers and deceivers, especially they of the circumcision: Whose mouths must be stopped, who subvert whole houses, teaching things which they ought not, for filthy lucre's sake." *Titus 1:10-11*

After the death of the Apostle Paul, there was virtually no one left among the Apostles, with the exception of Peter, who, had both the revelation, and the calling to teach these truths to the Gentile Church. Remember, Paul said the seven feasts were a rehearsal, or type and shadow of things to come. Much of the meanings of the three Spring Feasts have already been fulfilled by the death, burial, and resurrection of Jesus. When the Holy Spirit was poured out on the Church, and three thousand souls were baptized by the Spirit of God, the meaning of the Feast of Pentecost was fulfilled. The meanings of the three Fall Feasts, however have yet to be fulfilled by Jesus, and the last-days victorious Church. As stated earlier these three Fall Feasts are the Feast of Trumpets, also known as Yom Teruah or Rosh Hashana. The Day of Atonement, also known as Yom Kippur, and the Feast of Tabernacles, also known as Sukkot. Again, all three of these Fall Fests represent things in *Bible* prophecy that have not yet happened. Before we venture into discussing these seven feasts, we must again review, and understand the significance of the early and latter rains which Israel's agricultural seasons were totally dependent on. All of these feasts were connected to these rainy seasons and their subsequent crop harvests. Israel had two distinct rainy seasons every year, one in the spring, and one in the fall. If the early spring rains came on time some fast growing crops could be harvested twice each year. After a long hot summer the later rains would prepare the much larger fall harvest to be reaped. **"Be patient therefore, brethren, unto the coming of the Lord. Behold, the husbandman waiteth for the precious fruit of the earth, and hath long patience for it, until he receive the early and latter rain."** *James 5:7*

"Be glad then, ye children of Zion, and rejoice in the Lord your God: for he hath given you the former rain moderately, and he will cause to come down for you the rain, the former rain, and the latter rain in the

first month." *Joel 2:23*

The three Spring Feasts happened within the first week of Passover, while the fourth early summer Feast of Pentecost, happened almost two months later, or fifty days to be exact.

Feast # 1 is Passover, or Pesach, which is the first feast celebrated each year on the 14th day of the Jewish month of Nisan (March-April). **"In the fourteenth day of the first month at even is the Lord's passover."** *Leviticus 23:5*

The *Septuagint* states: **"In the first month, on the fourteenth day of the month, between the evening times is the Lord's passover."** *Leviticus 23:5*

The Hebrew word "pesach" means to jump, spring, or pass over something, thus we get the English word Passover, which announces the arrival of spring on the Jewish calendar. The Feast of Passover was meant to point the Children of Israel back to their deliverance from slavery in Egypt which was part of the promise in the Abrahamic Covenant. After serving as virtual slaves to Pharaoh, God would deliver his children after visiting on the Egyptians one last judgement, the death of their first born child. **"Then Moses said, Thus says the Lord:, About midnight will I will go out into the midst of Egypt: and all the firstborn in the land of Egypt shall die, from the firstborn of Pharaoh who sits on his throne, even unto the firstborn of the maidservant that is behind the mill; and all the first born of the beasts. Then there shall be a great cry throughout all the land of Egypt, such as there was none like it, nor shall be like it any more. But against any of the children of Israel shall not a dog move its tongue, against man or beast: that you may know how the Lord doeth put a difference between the Egyptians and Israel."** *Exodus 11:4-7*

To protect the Israelites from this last plague they were to choose a lamb for their Passover meal and apply its blood to the top and sides of their doorposts. When the angel of death saw the blood he would pass over their houses. This feast was meant to point the Jews each year, back to when they had killed the innocent Passover lamb, sprinkled its blood on their doorposts, and then ate the first Passover meal in haste, ready to depart Egypt. **"And the blood shall be to you for a token upon the houses where ye are: and when I see the blood, I will pass over you, and the plague shall not be upon you to destroy you, when I smite the land of Egypt."** *Exodus 12:13*

The lamb used by the Israelites had to be perfect, of the first year, without any blemishes or broken bones. The lamb had to be completely consumed that night, without anything left over. As the Israelites ate the lamb that night, every one of them was healed in body, and ready for their journey out of Egypt. **"He smote also all the firstborn in their land, the chief of all their strength. He brought them forth with silver and gold, and there was none feeble person among His tribes."** *Psalm 105:36-37*

"And it came to pass at the end of the four hundred and thirty years, even the selfsame day it came to pass, that all the host of the Lord went out from the land of Egypt. It is a night to be much observed unto the Lord for bringing them out from the land of Egypt: this is that night of the Lord to be observed of all the children of Israel in their generations." *Exodus 12:41-42*

The Feast Season of Passover was also meant to point the Jews forward to the death of Jesus, who was our true Passover Lamb. **"The next day John seeth Jesus coming unto him, and sayeth, Behold the Lamb of God, which taketh away the sin of the world."** *John 1:29*

The Holy, unblemished Lamb of God provided for our spirit, soul, and body in His death on the cross at Calvary. **"He was wounded for our transgressions, He was bruised for our iniquities; the chastisement for our peace was upon Him; and with His stripes we are healed."** *Isaiah 53:5*

The first Passover in Egypt took place in the seventh month (Abib or Nisan), of the old Jewish secular calendar. God then rescheduled the Jewish calendar so that from that time forward, the seventh month was changed to the first month, but the names of the months remained basically the same. **"And the Lord spake unto Moses and Aron in the land of Egypt, saying, This month shall be unto you the beginning of months: it shall be the first month of the year to you."** *Exodus 12:1-2*

Feast # 2 is Unleavened Bread, or Hag HaMatzah, which begins on the 15th day of the Jewish month of Nisan (March-April), and lasts for 7 days. **"And on the fifteenth day of the same month is the feast of unleavened bread unto the Lord: seven days you must eat unleavened bread."** *Leviticus 23:6*

"And they shall eat the flesh in that night, roast with fire, and un-

leavened bread; and with bitter herbs they shall eat it. Eat not of it raw, nor sodden at all with water, but roast with fire; his head with his legs, and with the appurtenance thereof. And ye shall let nothing of it remain until the morning; and that which remaineth of it until the morning ye shall burn with fire." *Exodus 12:8-10*

The *Septuagint* states: "**And on the fifteenth day of this month is the feast of unleavened bread to the Lord; seven days shall ye eat unleavened bread.**" *Leviticus 23:6*

"**And they shall eat the flesh in this night roast with fire, and they shall eat unleavened bread with bitter herbs. Ye shall not eat it raw nor sodden in water, but only roast with fire, the head with the feet and the appurtenance. Nothing shall be left of it till the morning, and a bone of it ye shall not break; but that which is left of it till the morning ye shall burn with fire.**" *Exodus 12:8-10*

The Feast of Unleavened Bread was meant to point the Children of Israel back to the meal they ate just before being delivered from Egypt. The Israelites had to flee Egypt so quickly that the bread in their ovens did not have time to rise, thus their bread was unleavened. Every spring Jewish women would search throughout their houses to assure there was no leaven left from the previous year before the Passover meal (seder meal) began. "**Seven days shall you eat unleavened bread; even the first day ye shall put away leaven out of your houses: for whosoever eateth leavened bread from the** first day until the seventh day, that soul shall be cut off from Israel." *Exodus 12:15*

Leaven, which can be either yeast, or baking powder, is always referred to in the *Bible* is a symbol, or type of sin and evil. For example the Apostle Paul states: "**Purge out therefore the old leaven, that ye may be a new lump, as ye are unleavened. For even Christ our Passover is sacrificed for us. Therefore let us keep the feast, not with old leaven, neither with the leaven of malice and wickedness; but with the unleavened bread of sincerity and truth.**" *I Corinthians 5:7-8*

When Jesus ate the Last Supper with his disciples, he told them the bread represented His body which would be broken for us all. "And as they were eating, Jesus took bread, and blessed it, and break it, and gave it to the disciples, and said, Take, eat; this is my body." *Matthew 26:26*

"And he took bread, and gave thanks and break it, and gave unto them, saying, This is my body which is given for you: do this in remembrance of me." *Luke 22:19*

The Feast of Unleavened Bread was originally meant to point the Jews forward in time to the death and burial of Jesus, and the three days and nights he spent in Abraham's Bosom. Jesus said: **"For as Johas was three days and three nights in the whale's belly; so shall the Son of man be three days and three nights in the heart of the earth."** *Matthew 12:40*

Jesus spent three days and nights preaching to the departed souls in Abraham's Bosom (read the whole 16th chapter of Luke), who were held there awaiting their resurrection. After Jesus preached the good news of the Kingdom of God, and was resurrected on the third day, many of these departed souls believed his gospel. Those who believed came up out of their graves with Jesus and went into the City of Jerusalem to appear to many of their living relatives. **"And the graves were opened; and many bodies of the saints which slept arose, And came out of the graves after his resurrection, and went into the holy city, and appeared unto many."** *Matthew 27:52-53*

Although Jesus was the first of the first fruits, I personally believe it was these resurrected Old Testament saints that the Apostle Paul referred to as the first fruits. **"For as in Adam all die, even so in Christ shall all be made alive. But every man in his own order: Christ the firstfruits; afterward they that are Christ's at his coming."** *I Corinthians 15:22-23*

Feast # 3 is First Fruits, or Bikkurim, or Reishit, which always occurs on the 16th day of Nisan (March-April) during the week of Unleavened Bread. **"Speak unto the children Israel, and say unto them, When ye be come into the land which I give unto you, and shall reap the harvest thereof, then you shall bring sheaf of the first fruits of your harvest unto the priest. And he shall wave the sheaf before the Lord, to be accepted for you: on the morrow after the sabbath the priest shall wave it."** *Leviticus 23:10-11*

The *Septuagint* states: **"Speak to the children of Israel, and thou shall say to them, When ye shall enter into the land which I give you, and reap the harvest of it, then shall you bring a sheaf, the first fruits of your harvest, to the priest; and he shall lift up the sheaf before the Lord, to be accepted for you."** *Leviticus 23:10-11*

The Feast of First Fruits is held on the Sunday immediately following the Feast of Unleavened Bread. The waving of the first sheaf of grain to ripen in Israel's fields was a type and shadow of Jesus Christ, the first born from the dead. Said another way, when the High Priest waved the first sheaf of grain before the Lord our God, it was meant to point the Children of Israel to the resurrection from the dead of our Lord Jesus Christ. Very early on Sunday morning (resurrection morning), Jesus appeared to Mary Magdalene in front of the empty sepulcher. As Mary approached Jesus to touch him, Jesus stopped her with a very mysterious explanation. Although Mary was later allowed to hold Jesus by the feet (*Matthew* 28:9), Jesus said to her: "Touch me not; for I am not yet ascended to **my father: but go to my brethren, and say unto them, I ascend unto my Father, and your Father; and to my God, and your God."** *John 20:17*

Again, Jesus told Mary the very reason not to touch him, because as our high priest, Jesus had to be ceremonially clean before he could ascend into heaven and cleanse the heavenly utensils of worship. **"But Christ being come an high priest of good things to come, by a greater and more perfect tabernacle, not made with hands, that is to say, not of this building; Neither by the blood of goats and calves, but by his own blood he entered in once into the holy place, having obtained eternal redemption for us."** *Hebrews 9:11*

"It was therefore necessary that the (earthly) **patterns of things in the heavens should be purified with these** (blood of bulls and goats); **but the heavenly things themselves** (was purified) **with better sacrifices than these. For Christ is not entered into the holy places made with hands, which are the figures** (patterns) **of the true; but into heaven itself, now to appear in the presence of God for us."** *Hebrews 9:23-24*

The Apostle Paul has just made a profound, and mysterious statement, in that the heavenly utensils of worship needed to be cleansed with Christ's blood. Why would something made in heaven, by God, need cleansing? Again, if all things made by God were good, why then was it necessary that the heavenly temple, and its mercy seat, need to be sprinkled, and cleansed with Christ's blood? There can be only one answer which points us all the way back to the Preadamite World. Lucifer was the "Anointed Cherub that covereth (possibly covered or controlled the Mercy Seat), in the Holy Mountain of God. **"Thou art the anointed cherub that covereth; and I** have set thee so: thou was upon the holy mountain of God; thou hast walked up and down in the midst of the stones of fire. Thou wast perfect in thy ways from the day that thou wast created, till iniquity was found in thee." *Ezekiel 28:14-15*

Although we are not told in the *Bible* of this incident, Lucifer must have somehow defiled the Mercy Seat, or the heavenly utensils of worship, during his prideful rebellion to God's authority.

The Feast of First Fruits was the last feast which Jesus fulfilled while on earth, before his final resurrection to heaven.

Feast # 4 is Pentecost, or Shavout, or Feast of Weeks, which always occurs on the 6th to the 7th day of Sivan (May-June), exactly 50 days after First Fruits, or Bikkurim. **"And ye shall count unto you from the morrow after the sabbath, from the day that you brought the sheaf of the wave offering; seven sabbaths shall be complete. Even unto the morrow after the seventh sabbath shall ye number fifty days; and ye shall offer a new meat offering unto the Lord."** *Leviticus 23:15-16*

The *Septuagint* states: **"And ye shall number to yourselves from the day after the sabbath, from the day on which you shall offer the sheaf of the heave-offering, seven full weeks: until the morrow after the last week ye shall number fifty days, and shall bring a new meat-offering to the Lord."** *Leviticus 23:15-16*

The Feast of Pentecost was meant to point the Children of Israel to the descent from Heaven of the Holy Spirit, and the birth of the Victorious Church on earth.

Feast # 5 is the Feast of Trumpets, or Yom Teruah, or Rosh Hashana, which always occurs on the 1st day of the Jewish month of Tishri (September-October). **"Speak unto the children of Israel, saying, In the seventh month, in the first day of the month, shall ye have a sabbath, a memorial of blowing of trumpets, an holy convocation."** *Leviticus 23:24*

The *Septuagint* states: **"Speak to the children of Israel, saying, In the seventh month, on the first day of the month, ye shall have a rest, a memorial of trumpets: it shall be to you a holy convocation."** *Leviticus 23:24*

The Fall Feast Season came during the Jewish month of Tishri which was at the end of the harvest season, thus it was sometimes referred to as the "Feast of Ingathering" (Exodus 23:16), in the *Bible*. The Feast of Trumpets was always celebrated by the blowing of a ram's horn, known as the shofar, throughout the land of Israel. Your author believes this feast was meant to point the Children of Israel to the Last Trumpet that will announce the second coming of Jesus, their true Messiah, back to this earth. The shofar was used to announce the coronation of a new king as in the case of King Solomon. **"And Zadok the priest took an horn of oil out of the tabernacle, and anointed Solomon. And they blew the trumpet; and all the people said, God save King Solomon."** *I Kings 1:39*

When Jesus returns to this earth a second time as Lord of Lords, and King of Kings, the shofar will sound again throughout Israel. **"And the Lord shall be seen over them, and his arrow shall go forth as the lightning: and the Lord God shall blow the trumpet, and shall go with whirlwinds of the south."** *Zechariah 9:14*

"That day is a day of wrath, a day of trouble and destress, a day of wasteness and desolation, a day of darkness and gloominess, a day of clouds and thick darkness, A day of the trumpet and alarm against the fenced cities, and against the high towers." *Zephaniah 1:15-16*

"Behold, I show you a mystery; We shall not all sleep, but we shall all be changed, In a moment, in the twinkeling of an eye, at the last trump: for the trumpet shall sound, and the dead shall be raised incorruptible, and we shall be changed." *I Corinthians 15:51-52*

"For the Lord himself shall descend from heaven with a shout, with the voice of the archangel, and with the trump of God: and the dead in Christ shall rise first." *I Thessalonians 4:15-16*

"And then shall appear the sign of the Son of man in heaven: and then shall all the tribes of the earth mourn, and they shall see the Son of man coming in the clouds of heaven with power and great glory. And he shall send his angels with a great sound of a trumpet, and they shall gather together his elect from the four winds, from one end of heaven to the other." *Matthew 24:30-31*

Feast # 6 is the Day of Atonement, or Yom Kippur, which always occurs on the 10th day of the Jewish month of Tishri (September-October). "And the Lord spake unto Moses, saying, Also on the tenth day of this seventh month there shall be a day of atonement: it shall be an holy day convocation unto you; and ye shall afflict your souls, and offer an offering made by fire unto the Lord. And you shall do no work in that same day: for it is a day of atonement, to make an atonement for you before the Lord your God. For whatsoever soul it be that shall not be afflicted in that same day, he shall be cut off from among his people. And whatsoever soul it be that doeth any work in that same day, the same soul will I destroy from among his people. Ye shall do no manner of work: it shall be a statute for ever throughout your generations in all your dwellings. It shall be to you a sabbath of rest, and ye shall afflict your souls: in the ninth day of the month at even, from evenunto even, shall ye celebrate your sabbath." *Leviticus 23:26-32*

The *Septuagint* states: "And the Lord spoke to Moses, saying, Also on the tenth day of this seventh month is a day of atonement: it shall be a holy convocation to you; and ye shall humble your souls, and offer a whole-burnt-offering to the Lord. Ye shall do no work on this self-same day: for this is a day of atonement for you, to make atonement for you before the Lord your God. Every soul that shall not be humbled in that day, shall be cut off from among its people. And every soul which shall do work on that day, that soul shall be destroyed from among its people. Ye shall do no manner of work: it is a perpetual statute throughout your generations in all your habitations. It shall be a holy sabbath to you; and ye shall humble your souls, from the ninth day of the month: from evening to evening ye shall keep your sabbaths." *Leviticus 23:26-32*

The Jews always celebrated the Feast of Atonement as the "Great Day of Cleansing", thus they sometimes referred to it as the "Day of Judgement." The Day of Atonement is the only required national-day of fasting recorded in the Old Testament. The Feast of Atonement was always celebrated as a time of godly repentance, and a contrite heart, in confessing the sins of the nation. The Day of Atonement was the one day in the year when the High Priest would be allowed to go behind the veil into the Holy of Holies, to sprinkle blood on the Mercy Seat. The word Atonement means to cover, thus the sins of the whole Jewish nation was covered for a full year by this blood sacrifice. "And he (The High Priest) shall make an atonement for the holy sanctuary, and he shall make an atonement for the tabernacle of the congregation, and for the alter, and he shall make an atonement for the priests, and for all the people of the congregation. And this shall be an everlasting statute unto you, to make an atonement for the children of Israel for all their sins once a year. And he did as the Lord commanded Moses." *Leviticus 16:33-34*

Today, on the day of Atonement, Jews from around the world gather in their synagogues, where they refuse anything to eat, or to do work of any kind. It is the personal belief of this author that the Feast of Atonement was meant to point the Children of Israel, in the last-days, to the fact that as a nation they had rejected their true Messiah. But by accepting Jesus's blood sacrifice on the cross, they could now be made clan in the eyes of God. This will be a day of bitter reflection and soul searching for the Jewish people who finally accept Jesus as their personal Messiah, and their personal savior from their sins. The ten days between the Feast of Trumpets, and the Feast of Atonement was always called the "Awesome Days of Repentance." When Jesus returns to earth the second time, the Feast of Atonement will again be celebrated in the same way. **"And I will pour upon the house of David, and upon the inhabitants of Jerusalem, the spirit of grace and of supplication: and they shall look upon me whom they have pierced, and they shall mourn for him, as one mornith for his only son, and shall be in bitterness for him, as one that is in bitterness for his first born."** *Zachariah 12:10*

"And it shall come to pass in that day, that the Lord shall set his hand again the second time to recover the remnant of his people, which shall be left, from Assyria, and from Egypt, and from Pathros, and from Cush, and from Elam, and from Shinar, and from Hamath, and from the islands of the sea. And he shall set up an ensign for the nations, and shall assemble the outcasts of Israel, and gather together the dispersed of Judah from the four corners of the earth." *Isaiah 11:-12*

"In those days, and in that time, saith the Lord, The children of Israel shall come. They and the children of Juda together, Going and weeping: they shall go, And seek the Lord their God." *Jeremiah 50:4*

"In those days, and in that time, saith the Lord, The iniquity of Israel shall be sought for, and there shall be none; And the sins of Judas, and they shall not be found: For I will pardon them whom I reserve." *Jeremiah 50:20*

Feast # 7 is the Feast of Tabernacles, or Sukkot, also known as the Feast of Booths, or the Feast of Nations, or the Feast of ingathering, which always occurs between the 15th to the 22nd day of the Jewish month of Tishri (September-October).

And ye shall keep it a feast unto the Lord seven days in the year. It shall be a statute forever in your generations: you shall celebrate it in the seventh month.

Ye shall dwell in booths seven days; all that are Israelites born shall dwell in booths. That your generations may know that I made the children of Israel to dwell in booths, when I brought them out of the land of Egypt: I am the Lord your God." *Leviticus 23:40-43*

The *Septuagint* states: "Speak to the children of Israel, saying, On the fifteenth day of this seventh month, there shall be a feast of tabernacles seven days to the Lord. And on the first day shall be a holy convocation; ye shall do no servile work. Seven days shall ye offer whole-burnt-offerings to the Lord, and the eighth-day shall be a holy convocation to you; and ye shall offer whole-burnt-offerings to the Lord: it is a time of release, ye shall do no servile work." *Leviticus 23:33-36*

The Septuagint further states: "And on the first day ye shall take goodly fruit of trees, and branches of palm trees, and thick boughs of trees, and willows, and branches of osiers from the brook, to rejoice before the Lord your God seven days in the year. It is a perpetual statute for your generations in the seventh month ye shall keep it. Seven days ye shall dwell in tabernacles; every native in Israel shall dwell in tents, that your posterity may see, that I made the children of Israel to dwell in tents, when I brought them out of the land of Egypt: I am the Lord your God." *Leviticus 23:40-43*

The Feast of Tabernacles was meant to point the Children of Israel, and later the New Testament Church, to the one-thousand year Millennial Reign of Christ here on earth. During this time we will be living with God, and he will again be living in the midst of his people. "And the Word was made flesh, and dwelt among us, and we beheld his glory, the glory as of the only begotten of the father, full of grace and truth." *John 1:14*

After Jesus returns to earth at the sounding of the last trump, he will gather to himself his bride, the Church. Not long after that King David will be giver authority to start build the Millennial Temple in Jerusalem, where he will reign as co-regent with Christ over the Twelve Tribes of Israel. "In those days, and at that time, will I cause the Branch of righteousness to grow up unto David; and he shall execute judgement and righteousness in the land." *Jeremiah 33:15*

During the Millennial Reign of Christ all nations will be required to observe all the feast including the Feast of Tabernacles. "And it shall come to pass that every one that is left of all the nations which came against Jerusalem shall even go up from year to year to worship the King, the Lord of hosts, and to keep the feast of tabernacles. And it shall be that whoever will not come up of all the families of the earth unto Jerusalem to worship the King, the Lord of hosts, even upon them shall be no rain. And if the family of Egypt go not up, and come not, that have no rain, there shall be plague, with which the Lord will smite the nations that come not up to keep the feast of tabernacles. This shall be the punishment of Egypt, and the punishment of all nations that come not up to keep the feast of tabernacles." *Zechariah 14:16-19*

Chapter 12

America's Pagan Capital

The Church of England published the Authorized Version of the *King James Bible* in 1611, just four years after the first English colony in North America was established at Jamestown Virginia in 1607. This *Bible* dominated the Puritan preaching in the first colonies, and the teaching and thinking of most English-speaking Americans for over the next three hundred years. Biblical names were given to people, towns, and counties throughout the original thirteen colonies, and later, throughout America. In cities like Boston, Philadelphia, and even New York, there are countless depictions, and monuments, dedicated to biblical themes. Even though many historians say that General George Washington was a deist, yet, we know he was well versed in both the new and old testaments of the King James Bible. Deism is an Age of Enlightenment Philosophy that teaches that although God had created everything in the universe, including man, God was distant, and unapproachable by mankind, and did not answer prayers, or perform miracles. Deists themselves describe their god as a kind of divine watchmaker, who created the world as a perfectly synchronized machine, then stepped away from it. Their god's secrets can only be revealed in nature, through the use of reason alone. The only one of the founding fathers that we know for sure to be a Deist was Thomas Paine, which is plainly stated in his book *The Age of Reason*. Some historians believe, as a young man, Benjamin Franklyn was also a Deist, but changed his beliefs later in life during the Christian revival known as the Great Awakening. It is said that in his later years Franklin was heavily influenced by the preaching of the British preacher George Whitfield, who, in 1770, held a series of revivals in New England. Franklin was the only one of our founding fathers to have signed all three of America's founding documents, the Declaration of Independence, the Treaty of Paris, and the US Constitution. Franklyn first met Paine while living in England and then helped him come to America. Franklin then helped Paine print his first book *Common Since*, which was the book which influenced most Americans to fight in the

Revolutionary War. When Paine later wrote *The Age of Reason*, American's were shocked to read his anti-Christian views. Paine was a talented writer who would have made a great speechwriter for the Antichrist. Washington's family name, went back seven generations in the Virginia Colony, to an English royalist on the run from Cromwell's victorious Puritan army after the English Civil War. Once established in America, the Washingtons became established members of the Anglican Church, which later became known as the Episcopalian Church. The Washington family church pew is still on display in Arlington Virginia. As a young man, Washington learned both Greek and Latin, thus he knew the difference between a Democracy, which was created by the Greeks, and a Republic, which was created by the Romans. Although he was well read by the time he was a man, Washington, loved, and read his *King James Bible*, more than anything else. In his personal letters and documents Washington quotes from the *King James Bible* more than two hundred times. If Washington was a deist, as many historians say, he was the best versed in the *King James Bible*, of all times. Whether he was a deist or not, we definitely know Washington was inducted into a masonic lodge in Fredericksburg, Virginia on November 4, 1752. The man most credited with bringing Masonry to America was a man named Daniel Cox, who was an English Mason, a member of Lodge No. 8 at Devil's Tavern in London. After living in the American colonies for a while, Cox traveled back to London to get a charter, authorizing him to found lodges throughout the American colonies. In 1730, Cox, just before his return to America was given his charter, declaring him to be the official Provincial Grand Master of North America. After returning to America, with his charter in hand, Cox traveled throughout the colonies, trying to organize various groups to found Masonic lodges. Cox organized Masonic lodges among the Pennsylvania Quakers, New York Dutch, New Jersey Scots, Delaware Swedes, and Massachusetts Puritans. After becoming a Freemason himself in in 1752, Washington, during the Revolutionary War, often encouraged his officers to become Freemasons. During the Revolutionary War, General George Washington also encouraged his solders, especially his officers to regularly read the 1769 revision of the *King James Bible*, yet we have no written record of him ever clearly stating, or confessing to having had a born-again conversion experience. This was also true of many of the other founding fathers who, like Washington were known to be either Rosicrucian's or Freemasons. As of the signing of the American Constitution in Philadelphia on 17 September 1787, nine of its signatories were confessed

Freemasons, and six more Masons would soon sign, placing their lives and fortunes in jeopardy against England. Why are there so many biblically in-spired statues and monuments in both Boston, and Philadelphia, and even some in New York City, yet most of the statues, paintings, and monuments in Washington D.C., are almost exclusively pagan inspired? Sadly, the an-swer to this question is that the anti-Christian pagans that first designed and built Washington D.C., are the same kind of anti-Christian pagans that control it to this day. This disconnect between the biblical concepts that dominated the thinking of most Americans during Washington's day, and the design and layout of the city that today bears his name, remains, to most people a mystery. Why is there literally dozens of carved depictions of Jahbulon, or Baal, strewn throughout the city? Why is the Greek Athenian Solon, and the Chinese Confucius, displayed on the pediment above the east entrance of our Supreme Court Building? Today, American Christians are slowly, but surely, coming to the realization that the iconography on both the inside, and outside of our capital buildings, do not represent that of a Christian nation. An example of this disconnect can be seen in the fact that the proposed design for the Great Seal of the United States, was noth-ing like it appears today. On July 4, 1776, the Continental Congress ap-pointed John Adams, Benjamin Franklin, and Thomas Jefferson to design the Great Seal. Franklin and Jefferson's plans were similar in that they both depicted the Children of Israel in the desert. Jefferson's design depicted the Israelites being led by a cloud by day and a pillar of fire by night. Franklin's design depicted the Israelites crossing the Red Sea, with Pharaoh's army in hot pursuit, with Moses standing on the other side. The proposed motto, of Franklin's design was to appear under the seal, and was to read: "Rebellion to Tyrants is Obedience to God." However John Adam's design was not biblical, but pagan, in that it featured Hercules leaning and resting on his club. Why then did we end up with a Great Seal, with an Egyptian phoenix (not an eagle) on one side, and the Great Pyramid of Giza, with the Eye of Nimrod/Osiris hovering above it on the other side? The answer to this question is that the Freemasons, who were in control of its design, believe the Nephilim built the Great Pyramid of Giza as a crypt, or tomb for the dead body of Nimrod. As I earlier stated in chapter three of this book, Osiris's spirit was thought, by the Egyptians, to have been resurrected onto one of the three stars, Alnitak, Alnilam, and Mintaka (see chapter three), which make up Orion's Belt. Osiris's dead body was then supposedly bur-ied somewhere inside the Great Pyramid of Giza, waiting to be resurrected.

The notorious 33rd Degree Freemason, and Satanist, Aliester Crowley, believed Nimrod was buried in the Great Pyramid of Giza, and often referred to his resurrection as the "New Age of Horus." Your author also personally believes the dead body of Nimrod was actually buried in the Great Pyramid, and that it is still there, patiently waiting, and watching, for his reappearance as the coming Antichrist. This is why the eye of Nimrod/Osiris, sets atop the unfinished pyramid on the back of the Great Seal of America, and also appears on the back of your one-dollar bills. Concerning the Egyptian phoenix-bird depicted on the front side of the Great Seal, author Rob Skiba, in his book *Babylon Rising* states: **"Therefore, it is important to note here that the phoenix is also directly related to Osiris. For according to Egyptian mythology, the phoenix is associated with the sun god. She is called the *Bennu*, which means "the Ascending One", and essentially represents the soul of Osiris, rising up out of the ashes of death."** I personally believe Nimrod, the first Antichrist mentioned in the *Bible*, will be the last Antichrist mentioned in the *Bible*. Said another way, the Antichrist mentioned in the *Old Testament*, will be the resurrected Antichrist, mentioned in the New Testament. Today there are dozens of depictions of Nimrod's Zodiac on display in Washington D.C., more than in most large cities of the world. There are also several dozen statues of various pagan-gods, and goddesses on display throughout the streets of Washington, almost even as many as in the city of Rome. The original landmass of Washington D.C. was sandwiched between the southern state of Virginia, and the northern state of Maryland. Washington D.C. is built next to the banks of the Potomac River, near what was originally the haunt of the Algonquin Indians. What we today call "Capitol Hill," was once the place the Algonquin Indians held their yearly tribal grand council meetings at the foot of what was then known as the Roman Hill, later to be called Jenkins Heights. Historians argue over how this hill got its original name because there are simply no accurate records that go back that far. The following story is probably a mixture of fact and fiction, thus I will convey the story and let you decide what, if any of it you believe. In 1663 this tract of land was owned by a man named Francis Pope, who was thought by the locals to have the gift of prophecy. Supposedly, Pope had a vision in which he saw a new, and more powerful capital, even than in ancient Rome, occupying the hill, which he called the Roman Hill, or "New Rome." In the vision Pope saw a great and splendid parliament house on top of the hill, surrounded my several other magnificent buildings. According to Pope, after seeing the vision, he then quickly bought the hill from an Algonquin Indian and then renamed the hill New Rome after that great Italian city built on seven hills. In the Maryland State Archives, at Annapolis, there is a deed, dated June 5, 1663, in the name of Francis Pope, showing a strip of land called Rome. As far as the rest of the story, no one knows for sure what part of the story might be true. This area was later officially called Hamburg by the Dutch gun maker named Jacob Funk, who later bought the land. After Funk's death this swampy region became better known as Funkstown, by the few residents who lived there. But, people living up and down the Potomac River usually referred to it simply as Foggy Bottom, by all the locals who hunted and fished there. George Washington had first stumbled across this piece of land, with the Tiber Creek running through it, while working as a surveyor during his youth. Within this ten square mile piece of property was the hill then known as Jenkin's Heights, which, was the same hill named by Francis Pope as the Roman Hill, or New Rome. Francis Pope liked to jokingly call himself the "Pope of Rome on the Tiber." Jenkin's Heights, or New Rome would later become the site which we today call Capital Hill. Could Francis Pope's vision have been true? George Washington knew America needed a national capital, but he wanted it to be free from the political influence of the leaders of both Philadelphia, and New York. The Northern colonies wanted the new capital to be built in either Trenton, Philadelphia, or New York, while the Southern colonies wanted it to be built in its present location. The earliest recorded mention of creating a national capital was made in a letter dated 1783, from Thomas Jefferson and James Madison to the governor of Virginia, Benjamin Harris. They both suggested to Harrison that a small tract of land in the neighborhood of George Town, on the Potomac River, should serve as the site for America's new national capital. George Washington, with the consent of Congress, eventually appointed two Freemasons to survey, and draw up building and street plans for the new capital city. In 1790, the job of surveying the ten-mile square (diamond shaped) piece of land went to a civil engineer Freemason named Major Andrew Ellicott, and his two brothers Benjamin, and Joseph. In 1791, the task of drawing up the building and street plans went to a French artist, and Freemason named Pierre Charles L'Enfant. L'Enfant was the son of a famous French painter who painted portraits of the French elite and royalty, including the King of France. L'Enfant had been educated under the tutelage of his father, at the prestigious Royal Academy of Painting and Sculpture in Paris. While living in Paris, L'Enfant was a member of the masonic lodge known as the Lodge of the Nine Sisters. The name of this lodge was taken from the nine daughters of Zeus (see nine muses in chapter 6), mentioned earlier. Thus we can deduct from this that Franklin, Jefferson, and L'Enfant, all had a classical education and were all three familiar with ancient pagan traditions. While serving as ambassadors to France, both Thomas Jefferson, and Benjamin Franklin were members of this same lodge. Other notable members of this lodge were John Paul Jones and the Marquis de Lafayette. In fact, Benjamin Franklin was not only a member of the Nine Sisters Lodge, but for two years (1779-1780), he served as its Worshipful Grand Master. Franklin was present, and assisted in the initiation of Voltaire in the Lodge of Nine Sisters on April 7, 1778. Even before Franklin had traveled from America, to France to negotiate a treaty of alliance (December 4, 1776) between America and France, Franklin had earlier founded his own lodge in 1734. Franklin gave himself the title of Provincial Grand Master of the Grand Lodge of Pennsylvania, which was also known as the Leather Apron Club. This name was later changed to the Junto Club, and eventually became known as the American Philosophical Society. Some historians believe this club was the same group of Rosicrucians Franklin had established in what is now known as the Germantown section of Philadelphia. This is probably true because Franklin was both a friend, and associate of most of the leaders of the Germantown Rosicrucian community such as Johann Conrad Beissel, Julian Friedrich Sachse, Gabriel Eckerling, and his three brothers Israel, Samuel, and Emanuel. Franklin did most of the printing for the various German Rosicrucian, and Freemason groups that were founded in Ephrata, Wissahickon, and Lancaster County, Pennsylvania. The most famous of these groups was the Epharata Rosicrucian Cult founded in Pennsylvania by Johannes Kelpius in 1694. Fleeing Germany because of the Catholic Habsburg Empire's, Thirty Year's War, Kelpius first founded a commune outside of Philadelphia, on the banks of the Wissahickon Creek, which they called their Tabernacle in the Forest. Following Kelpius's death from tuberculosis in 1708, leadership of the cult was later taken over by a man named Johann Conrad Beissel, who led the cult in building a much larger commune at Ephrata, in Lancaster County, Pennsylvania. It soon became well known throughout Europe, that Pennsylvania and New York were both locations where arcane religious cults could enjoy freedom of worship, thus several European cults migrated to America. Several of these emigrant cults settled in central New York, which later gained the name of the Burned-Over District. This name came from the abundance of occult activity, and, at the same time, the numerous Christian revivals that took place in this one small area of New York. The abundance of printing work from these various Rosicrucian groups, and European cults, led Franklin to publish Reverend John Anderson's famous *Constitutions of the Free Masons* in 1734, which was the first Masonic book ever printed in America. After accompanying the famous French Major General Lafayette, to America, to fight in the Revolutionary War, L'Enfant was injured in Savannah in 1779. After recovering, L'Enfant eventually became part of General George Washington's personal staff, where he remained until the end of the war. Known as a city planner and architect, L'Enfant was hired to redesign and enlarge what later became known as Federal Hall, located in New York. The Federal Hall building in New York City, became our nation's first official capital from 1785 to 1790, and was the location where George Washington's first inauguration was held. Starting back in 1774, the Continental Congress had met in several locations such as Philadelphia, Baltimore, Lancaster, York, Princeton, Annapolis, Trenton, and New York City, thus a permanent capital city was needed. General Washington then appointed three commissioners, Thomas Jefferson, David Stuart, and Daniel Carrol, to oversee the new project. After the 100 square mile plot of land was surveyed by Ellicott, and his assistants, the question of giving free plots of land to various Christian denominations to build churches was raised. Both Benjamin Franklin, and Thomas Jefferson were opposed to giving any church group free property, especially the Catholic Church. Benjamin Franklin stated: **"When a Religion is good, I conceive it will support itself; and when it does not support itself, and God does not take care to support it so that its Professors are obliged to call for help of the Civil Power, it is a sign, I apprehend, of its being a bad one."** Thomas Jefferson agreed with Franklin and then said of the Catholic Church: **"Millions of innocent men, women, and children, since the introduction of Christianity, have been burnt, tortured, fined, imprisoned; yet we have not advanced one inch toward uniformity. What has been the effect of coercion? To make one half of the world fools and the other half hypocrites."** When surveying the land for the new capital, topographical elevations of the land required L'Enfant to make constant changes to the layout of his buildings, and street plans. L'Enfant had originally wanted to call our Capital Building the "Congress House," and our White House the "Presidential Palace." These two buildings would set across from each other connected by a broad boulevard, which we today call Pennsylvania Avenue. Extending west of the Congress House and south to the Presidential Palace, L'Enfant designed two wide "Grand Avenues" which today is known as the National Mall. George Washington recoiled at the thought of living in a Palace, thus the Congress created a contest to redesign both buildings, which was won a man named James Hoban. Utilizing Hoban's designs, both buildings were tones down a bit, and the presidential Palace was later renamed the White House, after it had to be repainted after the British burned it down in 1814. Because the temperamental, and contentious, French artist was not happy with having to make all these changes, L'Enfant complained to both Washington, and Congress on several occasions. L'Enfant's arrogance, and constant complaining got him fired after only one year, in January, of 1792, after he demanded the dismantling of a brand new house, built by a prominent politician. However, most of L'Enfant's classical revival building designs, and strange street plains, including six inverted five pointed stars, or pentagrams, were kept and followed by Ellicott. Some of L'Enfant's other street designs included the Jewish Kabbalah's Sephiroth, or Tree of Life, two squares and compass, and two six pointed stars (read my book The Synagogue of Satan), otherwise known as Hexagrams. The job of designing Washington D.C., then fell to the Freemason's Washington National Monument Society. For well over a century, the building of Washington's monuments came in spurts of activity, followed by periods of inactivity caused by sporadic funding. The Washington National Monument Society was made up of a group of Luciferians who had earlier directed Enfant to lay out the design of the Capital Building in relation to the Washington Monument, in such a way as to emulate the pagan temple theme of Nimrod's standing phallus, and Semiramis's pregnant belly and woob, the dome. Author Tomas Horn, in his book *The Final Roman Emperior, The Islamic Antichrist.* states: **"The US capital has been called the "Mirror Vatican" due to the strikingly similar layout and design of its primary buildings and streets. This is no accident. In Fact, America's forefathers first named the capital city Rome. But the parallelism between Washington and the Vatican is most clearly illustrated by the Capital Building and dome facing the obelisk known as the Washington Monument, and at St. Peter's Basilica in the Vatican by a similar Dome facing a familiar Obelisk—both of which were, according to their own official records, fashioned after the Roman Pantheon, the circular Domed Rotunda dedicated to all pagan gods."** Nimrod's phallus, represented by the obelisk is mentioned in the *Old Testament*, which God showed to Ezekiel, and called the "image of jealousy." This obelisk was built just outside of the northern gate, known as the gate of the alter, near the entrance of the Temple in Jerusalem. God transported Ezekiel to Jerusalem, to be a first-hand witness of this pagan abomination. **"And he put forth the form of a hand, and took me by a lock of mine head; and the spirit lifted me up between the earth and the heaven, and brought me in the visions of God to Jerusalem, to the door of the inner gate that looketh toward the north, where was the seat of the image of jealousy, which provoketh to jealousy. And, behold, the glory of the God of Israel was there, according to the vision that I saw in the plain. Then said he unto me, Son of man, lift up thine eyes now the way toward the north. So I lifted up mine eyes the way toward the north, and behold northward at the gate of the alter this (obelisk) image of jealousy in the entry. He said furthermore unto me, Son of man, seest thou what they do? Even the great abominations that the house of Israel committeth here, that I should go far off from my sanctuary? But turn thee yet again, and thou shalt see greater abominations."** *Ezekiel 8:3-6*

From 1793 to 1799, George Washington, and the Freemasons attempted to raise money by various means such as lotteries, donations, property sales, and even stock options, but their success was sporadic. The Freemasons were constantly bullying and cajoling Congress into funding one project after another. After Ellicott, and Banneker had topographically surveyed the purposed ten-mile square piece of land, the cornerstone of the new Federal District, was laid on April 15, 1791. It was placed at Jones Point on the Potomac, by the Alexandria Lodge No. 22, where George Washington was made a member on August 4, 1753. After becoming a Freemason, Washington was later criticized by various clergy, and church leaders throughout the colonies. He was often asked if he, or any other American Freemasons had any connection with Adam Weishaupt's Bavarian Illuminati, which was created in 1776. One year before his death in 1799, Washington wrote a letter, dated October 24, 1798, addressed to one Reverend George Washington Synder, in which Washington stated: **"It was not my intention to doubt that the doctrines of the Illuminati, and the principles of Jacobinism had not spread in the United States. On the contrary, no one is more truly satisfied of this fact than I am.**

The idea that I meant to convey was, that I did not believe that the Lodges of Free Masons in this country had, as Societies, endeavored to

propagate the diabolical tenets of the first, or pernicious principles of the latter. That individuals of them may have done it, or that the founder or instrument employed to found the democratic Societies in the United States, may have had these objects—and actually had a separation of the people from their Government in view, is too evident to be questioned."

The cornerstone of the construction of what would later become known as the White House was laid in the southwest corner of the foundation on Saturday, October 13, 1792. George Washington could not attend the dedication ceremony, thus a mason by the name of Peter Casanave presided over the ceremony in Washington's place. This procession of Masons, including its designer James Hoban, first gathered at the Fountain Inn in Georgetown, then marched together to the newly excavated site and performed the consecration ceremony. The following year, construction of America's Capital Building was officially started on September 17, 1793, located on Jenkin's Hill, the city's highest point. The hand chiseled cornerstone was prepared to be laid on its northeast corner by Freemasons from two different lodges, which included the buildings designers Dr. Willian Thornton, Thomas Walter, and Benjamin Latrobe. The next day, on Wednesday, the 18th, a large group of Freemasons, led by George Washington, dressed in full Masonic garb and regalia, consecrated the new building by means of a sacrifice of corn, oil, and wine. George Washington's famous embroidered masonic apron, was given to him by the Marquis de Lafayette, in August of 1784. On that land today there is a three-story structure with a nineteen foot tall cast bronze statue of Semiramis (see back cover) atop its dome, which we unashamedly today call our Capital Building. The ides of placing this statue atop the Capital dome came from its architect, Thomas U. Walter, who was, as you might expect, a Freemason. If you climb to the top of the stairs of the Capital Building, and look to your right, you will see a statue of Nimrod. The tour guides will tell you this is a statue of the Roman god Mars, the father of both Remus, and Romulus, the two founders of the ancient city of Rome, but it is in truth Nimrod. When you enter the Capital Building through the doors of its visitor's center you are greeted by the original nineteen foot sculpture of Semiramis, created by a Freemason named Thomas Crawford. "This was the original model for the Armed Statue of Freedom," as the Freemason's call it, which sets outside, atop the dome of the Capital Building. Inside this dome are depictions of several pagan-gods such as Neptune, Ceres, Minerva, Columbia, Vulcan, and Mercury. Where is Abraham, Moses, Jesus, or his twelve disciples? Upon entering the Rotunda of the dome you see many statues of past presidents, and around the base of the dome you see various scenes of American history from Columbus, through the Wright Brothers. Inside the dome is a fresco painted by the artist Constantino Brumidi, entitled the Apotheosis of Washington, which depicts the apotheosis, or deification of George Washington. Brumidi was an Italian painter who worked for the Jesuits, restoring paintings for them around the world. In 1849, Brumidi immigrated to America where he began working for the Jesuits, and the Knights of Malta, throughout America, but mostly on the east coast. Brumidi was commissioned to paint the fresco inside the dome of the Rotunda by Quartermaster General Montgomery C. Meigs, who was supervising the construction of the dome. Meigs was the Freemason in charge of pulling together all the artists and sculptors needed to finish out all the construction of the Capital Building. Inside the dome is a fresco which is meant to represent the womb of Isis. Around the outer ring of this fresco are several panels depicting scenes of Science, Agriculture, War, Commerce, and Naval battles. In the middle of the fresco is a depiction of George Washington, as a god, seated on his throne, with two woman seated on each side of him. One of these women supposedly represents victory and fame, while the other represents liberty. Around them are another thirteen women who represent the thirteen angels that was to usher Washington into the gates of heaven. These women are holding a banner which reads "*E Pluribus Unum*", which also appears on our Great Seal. Most people have been told this means "out of many one," but some Freemasons know its real interpretation reads: "one god (Washington) representing many." Yes, the Freemasons wanted all Americans to see Washington, after his death on December 14, 1799, as a reincarnated god (Mahatmas), or Ascended Master, thus, this is why many Freemasons originally called the Capital Building, the Temple of Liberty. You must understand that both the Freemasons, and the Rosicrucian's believe that George Washington was an "Ascended Master," who had been reincarnated in order to bring us hidden knowledge. Proof of this fact was plainly on display for almost a year when, Montgomery Meigs, the supervisor over the construction of the Capital Dome, placed a statue directly under the rotunda. This statue depicted George Washington as the Pagan-god Zeus setting on his throne. Congress had commissioned its sculptor Horatio Greenough to create a respectful image of Washington, seated at the Constitutional Convention. What they got for their money was so pagan, so over the top, and so offensive to Christians, that it was almost immediately removed to the National Museum of American History, where it remains to this day. Known as the American Zeus, Greenough's statue depicted a naked Washington, wrapped in what looks like a large beach towel, with one finger pointing upwards (as above, so below), and another finger pointing downward. The statue in fact, was an exact replica of the original forty-foot tall statue of the Olympian Zeus, carved by the Greek sculptor Phidias in 435 B.C. On the floor directly below the Capital Dome is an area known as "The Crypt," with forty columns supporting the Rotunda above. Directly below the dome, in the middle of the floor of the Crypt, is the Rosicrucian's rose-cross-compass, which supposedly marks the geographical center point of Washington D.C. Historian and author Tomas Horn, in his book *Apollyon Rising* states: **"Once you understand that Rosicrucianism (the inner doctrine of Masonry) is the mingling of Christianity with paganism, many of the founding fathers make more sense. A Rosicrucian can readily quote the Bible and make references to Christ, Jesus, the Savior, and so forth, but he will also exalt the teachings of Plato and the philosophers of old, and will look upon the gods of the ancient world as examples of virtue and justice."** On the floor directly below the Crypt is Washington's "empty tomb," which was originally built to house the body of Washington. Because Washington had stated clearly in his will that he wanted his mortal remains to be buried at Mount Vernon, this idea was later dropped. Before his death George Washington, and his masonic friends also laid the cornerstone of the White House on October 13, 1792, just seven years before his death in 1799. Two freemasons, Robert mills, and James Hoban, working in conjunction with Thomas Jefferson, designed and oversaw the building of the White House. Today the street grid of Washington D.C, is centered around the so-called Federal Triangle, which runs from the Capital building, west to the Jefferson Pier, then north to the White House before turning south and east again, back to the Capital Building. L'Enfant had originally envisaged the Washington Monument to have been built on the location known as the Jefferson Pier, but the location was eventually moved by orders from the Freemasons.. Starting in 1832, the Freemasons started raising money for the project, until by July 4, 1848, construction started on the monument after they had raised $87,000. Only six years later, in 1854, construction came to a complete halt after money for the new project dried up. Raising money to build the Washington Monument was rough with difficulty because of America's first third party, known as the Anti-Masonic Party, who opposed the Freemasons who were behind its construction. This first third party came into existence in 1828 because of the assassination of Captain William Morgan on September 11, 1826, which was planned in the two towns of Batavia and Canandaigua, New York. Morgan had written a book, in which he was going to reveal the Grand Omnific Royal Arch's word for the Freemasons true god, their "Architect of the Universe," which is Jahbulon, or Lucifer. These Freemasons knew that if the closely guarded Luciferian secrets of the Freemasons ever got out to the general public, there would literally be hell to pay. Captain Morgan had once been a Mason, but resigned after learning their true god was Lucifer, thus his book was entitled *Illustrations of Freemasonry by: One of the Fraternity.* As the title suggests, Morgan had been involved with the Masonic conspiracy before becoming a Christian and having a change of heart and exposing their Luciferic agenda. By breaking his oath of secrecy, Morgan had broken the Mason's cardinal law of secrecy, and thus, had signed his own death sentence. Several suspects from the Canandaigua Grand Lodge of New York, were ultimately detained, and questioned about the murder, but all were protected and defended by their individual Masonic lodges. Morgan had elevated himself into the secret Liciferic degrees, where he had learned the real god of the Mason's was Lucifer, not Jehovah. Morgan had made the mistake of showing part of his manuscript to a publisher who, in turn, revealed the book's content to the Freemasons. As Morgan's book drew closer to publication the publisher's print shop was burnt to the ground. Then on the 10th of September 1826, Morgan was arrested on a false charge of stealing a two-dollar shirt, and thrown in jail by a sheriff, and deputies, who were all Masons. Morgan's home was then searched and his manuscripts were seized and destroyed. Morgan was discharged two days later, but, on his way home, was abducted, then forcibly thrown into a carriage, by three men, and again thrown in jail. Sheriff Bruce, and his deputies, were Washington, D.C., which is the headquarters of the Southern Jurisdiction of the Scottish Rite. The imposing façade of this building is guarded by two seventeen-ton Egyptian sphinxes, and is said by some to contain over five-hundred million dollars, worth of Egyptian treasures, and supposed to assassinate Morgan, but, they also had a change of heart and could not carry out the death sentence. The investigation of the murder finally revealed that after Sheriff Bruce had backed out of the assassination plan, Morgan was then taken to Fort Niagara, where he was left in charge of a Colonel King. Colonel King, along with three deputies named Cheesboro, Sawyer, and Lawson, were then ordered to carry out the assassination from a boat, near where the Niagara River empties into Lake Ontario. The three assassins, after cutting his throat, then weighted down Morgan's body, and threw him overboard. The three assassins then reported back to Colonel King, saying "Morgan had justly met a traitor's doom." For his part in the assassination, Colonel King was held in Leavenworth Prison, but was mysteriously poisoned, and died, just before he was set to go on trial. Several Masons fled from New York, to Canada before they were forced to testify. Because there was no body, the three deputies were convicted only of kidnaping, thus they spent their misdemeanor convictions in minimum security prisons. The three deputies were confined in large carpeted cells, where their wives could permanently live with them. Strangely enough, after his assassination, Captain Morgan's wife Lucinda, eventually married Joseph Smith in 1836, the founder of Mormonism. Lucinda helped Joseph Smith found a Masonic lodge at his cult-community in Nauvoo Illinois. When a newspaper in Nauvoo started criticizing Smith, his followers sacked, burned, and destroyed much of the newspapers equipment, thus Smith was arrested in Carthage Illinois. Smith, and his Mormon followers were not trusted by the Protestant political establishment in the State of Illinois, thus the Mormons found themselves without the protection that the state's governor had earlier promised. An armed group of angry Protestants circled the two-story Carthage jailhouse on the evening of June 27, 1844, and shot the thirty-eight year old so-called prophet to death. After Joseph Smith was assassinated, Lucinda left Mormonism and became a Sister of Charity in the Catholic Church. When the full truth of the assassination of Captain Morgan finally leaked out to the general public, a backlash accrued because it was not the first incident of Masonic initiated murder. A young man named Daniel Rees was killed during a mock imitation ceremony when a pan of burning brandy was thrown into his face, whereupon he died three days later. When a portion of the manuscript of Morgan's book was finally discovered, and read, it was the final straw that broke the camel's back. This kicked off a mass exodus, starting in New York, and Philadelphia, which eventually caused the vast majority of America's Masons to abandon their lodges. Within one decade of Morgan's assassination, nine-tenths of American masons had renounced Freemasonry, and abandoned their lodges, thus Masonry almost disappeared in America. Soon, fifty-two anti-masonic newspapers appeared almost over-night, such as the *Anti-Freemason*, the *Boston Free Press*, the *An-*

ti-Masonic Baptist Herald, and the *Anti-Masonic Christian Herald.* Anti-masonic spelling, and math books were then released into America's schools, followed by the opening of a number of anti-masonic bookstores, throughout the east coast. Dozens of anti-Masonic representatives were elected to state legislatures. Feelings against the Freemasons grew to such an extent that there spring up a large number of anti-masonic taverns throughout the country, in which former masons were bared entrance. After the Anti-Masonic Party was formed, in 1831, it elected a presidential candidate named Wirt, whose candidacy split Andrew Jackson's opposition, thus, allowing Jackson to later win the presidency. After that, nothing in Washington D.C. which was known to be associated with the Freemasons, such as the Washington Monument, could not successfully be financed by the general public. With money dried up, construction of the Washington Monument stopped in 1855 at the 155-foot level and didn't restart again until 1876, when Congress finally appropriated two million dollars to get the construction started again. During the Civil Wars years, the area around the unfinished monument, became a slaughterhouse, to feed the Union troops. As far as the financial contributions needed to finish the project was concerned, it was not until after the Civil War, starting in 1879, that the general public once again began to contribute money to finish the Washington's Monument. Contributions would not have started again even at that time, had the general public not been lied to when they were told that the construction project had been taken away from the Freemasons, and handed over to the Union Army. The real truth was the Union Army, after the assassination of Abraham Lincoln were just following the orders and directions of the Ancient and Accepted Scottish Rite of Freemasons. The undisputed leader of this group of Luciferian-Freemasons was the confederate General Albert Pike, who in 1859 was elected its Sovereign Grand Commander of the Scottish Rite of Freemasonry's Southern Jurisdiction. This ceremony took place in Charleston, South Carolina, at what is known as the "Mother Lodge of the World." Pike, for thirty-two years literally controlled just about everything that happened in Washington D.C., until his death on April 2, 1892, at the age of 81. During these years Pike oversaw the finishing of both the Capital Building, and the Washington Monument, when its aluminum capstone, which the Freemasons call the Bin Bin, was set atop the monument on December 6, 1884. Pike also directed, and personally oversaw the beginning construction, and cornerstone ceremonies of many of Washington's other major buildings. Just before Abraham Lincoln was assassinated, he told his wife that after the Civil War was over, the one man he wanted to arrest, and bring up on charges of treason was General Albert Pike. After Lincoln's assassination Pike was arrested, tried, and convicted of treason, but was later pardoned and released from prison by President, Andrew Johnson, who was himself a Freemason. Pike was a recognized genius (read my book *Lucifer's Children*), who spoke almost a dozen languages, and who developed most of the dogmas, and rituals of the Scottish Rite. As head of the Supreme Council of the Scottish Rite, Pike laid out these dogmas and rituals in 1871, when he published his eight hundred page book, *Morals and Dogma of the Ancient and Accepted Scottish Rite of Freemasonry.* Today Pikes' body is buried in Washington at The House of the Temple at 1733 16th Street NW. Because Pike's body is buried there, there have been repeated threats to the building by several groups of people which have included both Christians and Muslims. For example, in March 2006, a Pakistani college student by the name of Syed Haris Ahmed, was arrested after making a video of the building, then giving it to al-Qaida, hoping the terrorists would bomb the building. He later told the FBI, he believed the Freemasons were "like the devil." There is a bronze statue of Albert Pike in Washington at Third and D Street Northwest, which has been defaced and vandalized several times by those who don't appreciate the following statements he made about his god Lucifer. Pike, talking about the *Book of Revelations,* stated: **"Seven trumpets to sound, and Seven cups to empty. The Apocalypse is, to those who receive the nineteenth Degree, the Apothesis of the Sublime Faith which aspires to God alone, and despises all the pomps and works of Lucifer. Lucifer, the light bearer! Strange and mysterious name to give to the Spirit of Darkness! Lucifer, the Son of the Morning! Is it he who bears the Light, and with its splendors intolerable binds feeble, sensual or selfish souls? Doubt it not!"** Page 321 of *Morals and Dogma.*

In conclusion are two very long, but very revealing statement made by Albert Pike. The first is addressed to the Great White Lodge, the High Priests of the Luciferian Brotherhood. To the leaders of the twenty-three Supreme Confederated Councils of the New and Reformed Palladian Rite. Albert Pike, on July 14, 1889 stated: **"That which we must say to the crowd is we worship god, but it is the god that one adores without superstition. To you, Sovereign Grand Inspector General, we say this, that you may repeat it to the Brethren of the 32nd, 31st, and 30th degrees. The Masonic Religion should be by all of us initiates of the high degrees, maintained in the purity of the Luciferian Doctrine. If Lucifer were not god, would Adonay (Jehovah) whose deeds prove** his cruelty, perfidy and hatred of men, barbarism and repulsion for science, would Adonay and his priests, calumniate him? Yes, Lucifer is God, and unfortunately Adonay is also god. For the eternal law is that there is no light without darkness, no beauty without ugliness, no white without black, for the absolute can exist only as two god's; darkness being necessary to light to serve as its foil as the pedestal is necessary to the statue, and the brake to the locomotive. In alogical and universal dynamics one can only lean on that will resist. Thus the universe is balanced by two forces which maintain its equilibrium: the force of attraction and that of repulsion. The two forces exist in physics, philosophy, and religion. And the scientific reality of the divine dualism is demonstrated by the phenomena of polarity and by the universal law of sympathies and antipathies. That is why the intelligent disciples of Zoroaster as well as, after them, the Gnostics, the Manicheans, and the Templars have admitted, as the only logical metaphysical conception, the system of two divine principles fighting eternally, and the one cannot believe the other inferior in power to the other. Thus the doctrine of Satanism is a heresy, and the true and pure philosophical religion is the belief in Lucifer, the equal of Adonai. But Lucifer, God of light and God of good, is struggling for humanity against Adonai (Jehovah), the God of darkness and evil."

This second quote by Pike comes from a letter written by Albert Pike, to Giuseppi Mazzini, head of the Illuminati of Europe, dated 1871, concerning the pure doctrine of Lucifer.

"We shall unleash the Nihilists, and the Atheists, and shall provoke a formidable social cataclysm which in all its horror will show clearly to the nations the effect of absolute atheism, origin of savagery, and of the most-bloody turmoil. Then everywhere, the citizens, obliged to defend themselves against the world minority of revolutionaries, will exterminate those destroyers of civilization, and the multitude, disillusioned with Christianity, whose deistic spirits will be from that moment without compass, anxious for an ideal, but without knowing where to render its adoration, will receive the universal manifestation of the pure doctrine of Lucifer brought finally out in the public view, a manifestation which will result from the general reactionary movement which will follow the destruction of Christianity and atheism, both conquered and exterminated at the same time."

This letter is catalogued in the British Museum Library of London, England

Chapter 13

The Sun-Clothed Woman

Satan's final attempt to kill her through the Antichrist's army, but they will emerge triumphant. **"And to the woman were given two wings of a** Throughout the *Bible* there is a theological principal known as the double witness. For example, in Egypt, Pharaoh's two dreams revealed seven plentiful harvests followed by seven lean years of famine. Joseph explained to the Pharaoh that because the thing was established by God, it was doubled unto him twice.

"And for that the dream was doubled unto Pharaoh twice; it is because the thing is established by God, and God will shortly bring it to pass." *Genesis 41:32*

In the prophecies of Daniel in the *Old Testament* the same principal applies to Nebuchadnezzar's dream recorded in the second chapter, and the parallel prophecy recorded in the seventh chapter. Both prophecies speak of the same thing, although different symbols are used to give additional details. In the *New Testament,* the same double mention principal applies in the *Book of Revelation* which is divided into two distinct parts. The first eleven chapters give us the entire apocalyptic story ending with the death and resurrection of the Two Witnesses. Then there is the sounding of the seven Trumpet Judgements which announces the Second Coming of Christ, and the beginning of the one-thousand year Millennium, which is celebrated by the Feast of Tabernacles. During the Millennial Kingdom, those who chose not to go to Jerusalem each year to celebrate the Feast of Tabernacles will be punished. The seventh, or Last Trumpet will sound at the end of the seven year tribulation period, on the Feast of Trumpets (Rosh Hashanah), and will announce the Post-Tribulation Rapture. **"Immediately <u>after the tribulation</u> of those days shall the sun be darkened, and the moon shall not give her light, and the stars shall fall from heaven, and the powers of the heavens shall be shaken. And then shall appear the sign of the Son of man in heaven: and then shall all the tribes of the earth mourn, and** they shall see the Son of man coming in the clouds of heaven (this is not a secret rapture where people do not know what has happened) **with power and great glory. And he shall send his angels with a great <u>sound of a trumpet</u>, and they shall gather together his elect from the four winds, from one end of heaven to the other.**" *Matthew 24:29-31*

"**Behold, I shew you a mystery; We shall not all sleep, but we shall all be changed, In a moment, in the twinkling of an eye, <u>at the last trump: for the trumpet shall sound</u>, and the dead shall be raised incorruptible, and we shall be changed.**" *I Corinthians 15:51-52*

"**For if we believe that Jesus died and rose again, even so them also which sleep in Jesus will God bring with him. For this we say unto you by the word of the Lord, that we which are alive and remain unto the coming of the Lord shall not prevent them which are asleep, For the Lord himself shall descend from heaven with a shout, with the voice of the archangel, and with <u>the trump of God</u>: and the dead in Christ shall rise first.**" *I Thessalonians 4:14-16*

"<u>**Blow ye the trumpet**</u> **in Zion, and sound an alarm in my holy mountain: let all the inhabitants of the land tremble: for the day of the Lord cometh, for it is nigh at hand.**" *Joel 1:1*

"**And <u>the seventh angel sounded</u>; and there were great voices in heaven, saying, The kingdoms of this world are become the kingdoms of our Lord, and of his Christ; and he shall reign for ever and ever.**" *Revelation 11:15*

During the sounding of the seventh trumpet our Lord Jesus Christ returns to this earth to rule and rain for a thousand years. The whole apocalyptic story is then retold a second time, starting in the twelfth chapter, but with additional symbols and details. These two corresponding chronological outlines coordinate, and harmonize the end-time mysteries God revealed to the Apostle John. The second chronological outline of the apocalyptic story starts again with the revelation of a heavenly pregnant woman ready to be delivered. Said another way, the first mystery revealed in the twelfth chapter of the *Book of Revelation* is the sign and symbol known as the Woman Clothed with the Sun. "**And there appeared a great wonder in heaven; a woman clothed with the sun, and the moon under her feet, and upon her head a crown of twelve stars: And she being with child cried, travailing in birth, and pain to be delivered. And there appeared** another wonder in heaven: and behold a great red dragon, having seven heads and ten horns, and seven crowns upon his head. And his tail drew a third part of the stars of heaven, and did cast them to the earth: and the dragon stood before the woman which was ready to be delivered, for to devour her child as soon as it was born. And she brought forth a manchild , who was to rule all nations with a rod of iron: and her child was caught up to God, and to his throne." *Revelation 12:1-5*

The word wonder is used twice in this passage of scripture, once in reference to the Sun-Clothed Woman, and once again in reference to the Great Red Dragon. This word wonder is translated from the Greek word semeion, which means a sign or symbol. This Greek word occurs thirty-one times in the gospels of Matthew, Mark, and Luke, where it is translated by the English words miracle, and sign. As to the interpretation of this sign-woman, some *Bible* scholars teach she is a symbol of the Church, and others teach she is a symbol of Israel, while the Catholic Church believes she represents the Virgin Mary. As we investigate these various signs and symbols we shall discover the sign-woman's true identity represents the fulfillment of the woman and her promises seed. The Great Dragon standing before the woman is Satan shown as having seven heads and ten horns. The sign of the dragon's crowns are a symbol representing seven successive pagan-world empires throughout history which Satan ruled over after Noah's Flood. These seven world-empires are Egypt, Assyria, Babylon, Media-Persia, Greece, Rome, and a revived Roman Empire which is in the making today. **"And here is the mind which hath wisdom. The seven heads are seven mountains** (world empires-high above all others), **on which the woman sitteth. And there are seven kings** (basileus-aristocracy or political-world rulers or world-emperors): **five are fallen** (Egypt, Assyria, Babylon, Meda-Persia, Greece)**, and one is** (Nero's Roman Empire of John's day)**, and the other** (revived pagan-empire) **is not yet came; and when it** (Egypt) **cometh, he** (Nimrod/Osiris, the originator of all pagan inspired religions) **must continue a short space. And the beast that was** (alive)**, and is not** (now dead)**, even he** (Nimrod/Osiris) **is the eighth, and is of the seven** (previous pagan-empires)**, and goeth** (will be judged and thrown into the lake of fire) **into perdition."** *Revelation 17:9-11*

"Here is wisdom. Let him that hath understanding count the number of the beast: for it is the number of a man; and his number is Six hundred threescore and six." *Revelation 13:18*

In Washington D.C., The freemasons erected the Washington Monument, not so much in memory of General George Washington, but to honor Nimrod/Osiris's lost penis. This obelisk rises to a height of 6,666 inches high, and is 666 inches wide on each of its four sides, at its base. In my opinion, the first antichrist recorded in the *Bible*, will be the last antichrist recorded in the *Bible*. I believe the last world empire will be headed by Nimrod/Osiris, who will be resurrected out of his underworld kingdom, to then take possession of the Antichrist. The freemasons believe Nimrod is buried in a secret chamber, somewhere inside the Great Pyramid of Giza, and will one day resurrect himself, followed by great signs and wonders. **"For there shall arise false Christs, and false prophets, and shall shew great signs and wonders; insomuch that, if it were possible, they shall deceive the very elect. Behold, I have told you before. Wherefore if they shall say unto you, Behold, he is in the desert; go not forth: behold, he is in the secret chambers; believe it not."** *Matthew 24:24-26*

Could that desert be in Egypt, and could that secret chamber be inside the Great Pyramid of Giza, depicted on the back of your one-dollar bills? Could the eye staring at you from atop the pyramid be the eye of Nimrod/Osiris? The answer to all three questions is yes. I am not the only one who believes that Nimrod will be the Antichrist. Researcher, and author Rob Skiba, in his book *Babylon Rising*, states: **"Jesus Christ is both God and man. He and Nimrod were both known as the King of kings and Lord of lords. Both have a cross (the Ankh) as their symbol. Both are known as a dying and resurrecting figure (though Nimrod has yet to do so). One is the Christ. One is the Antichrist, whose "god-number" just so happens to calculate out to 66.6% or 666 (in more ways than one). Jesus said He is the Alpha and Omega---the beginning and the end. Could it be that Nimrod was the first (anti-Christ) and that he will also be the last?"** The ten horns on the Great Dragon represents ten Moslem kindomless-kings (read my books *The Synagogue of Satan* and *Lucifer's Children*), who give their united power and authority unto the Antichrist which brings him to power. **"And the ten horns which thou sawest are ten kings** (basileis-aristocracy or political-world leaders, or world-emperors), **which have received no kingdom as yet; but receive power as kings one hour with the beast** (Antichrist). **These have one mind, and shall give their power and strength unto the beast. These shall make war with the Lamb, and the Lamb shall overcome them: for he is Lord of lords, and King of kings:**

and they which are with him are called, and chosen, and faithful." *Revelation 17:12-14*

"For God hath put it in their (the ten kings) hearts to fulfill his will, and agree, and give their (Moslem) kingdom unto the beast (Antichrist), until the words of God shall be fulfilled." *Revelation 17:17*

The sign-woman is a representation or symbol of the Seed-Woman who has stood against Satan throughout history, going all the way back to the Garden of Eden. Her Manchild represents Jesus, the rock cut out without hands seen in Daniel, the promised seed that will ultimately destroy Satan's seventh successive world empire. "Thou sawest till that a stone was cut out without hands, which smote the image upon his feet that were of iron and clay, and brake them to pieces." *Daniel 2:34*

The enmity between Satan and the Seed-Woman goes all the way back, even before the Egyptian World Empire, back to the Garden of Eden. "And I will put enmity between thee and the woman, and between thy seed and her seed; it shall bruise thy head and thou shalt bruise his heel." *Genesis 3:15*

In other words the imagery of the Sun Clothed Woman, represents God's covenant people throughout time including the twelve Patriarchs of Israel (see *Genesis* 37:9-11), all the way to the time of Christ. The sun, moon, and crown of twelve stars speaks of Joseph's dream, which was a forecast of future prophetic events. The crown of twelve stars upon the Woman's head also speaks of the twelve constellations, or Mizzaroth, in which the gospel of the Promised Seed was revealed for all to see in the heavens. Christ is promised as coming to Israel as the sun of righteousness (*Malachi* 4:2) with healing in his wings. Jesus came forth from Israel which is represented in *Isaiah* as travailing in birth to deliver a Manchild. "Before she travailed, she brought forth; before her pain came, she was delivered of a man child." *Isaiah 66:7*

"But when the fullness of the time was come, God sent forth his son, made of a woman, made under the law." *Galatians 4:4*

There can be no doubt as to the identity of the Manchild for Jesus is to receive all power and authority in both heaven and earth. The Manchild is to rule all nations with a rod of iron, which is exactly what is prophesied of him in the Psalms: "**Ask of me, and I shall give thee the heathen for thine inheritance, and the uttermost parts of the earth for thy possession. Thou shalt break them with a rod of iron; thou shalt dash them in pieces like a potter's vessel.**" *Psalms 2:8-9*

At the same time the Manchild is caught up to heaven, Satan and his fallen angels are cast down to earth. At this present time Satan still has access to the heavenlies (read *Ephesians* 6:12), thus we must conclude the fulfillment of this eviction did not take place at the ascension of Christ. We must also conclude that Satan's eviction from heaven will take place sometime in the near future. Some Bible scholars believe this will happen just before the beginning of the seven-year tribulation period, while other scholars believe it will happen in the middle of the tribulation period. "**And there was war in heaven: Michael and his angels fought against the dragon; and the dragon fought and his angels, and prevailed not; neither was their place found any more in heaven.** *Revelation 12:7-8*

Regardless of when this eviction takes place, the important thing for Christians to understand is that it will not take place until Christians exercise their authority which reaches all the way into the second heavens.

When this eviction from heaven to earth finally happens, Satan is enraged because he knows his time is short. Mankind at this time will face a time of great tribulation such as never happened before. "**Therefore rejoice, ye heavens, and ye that dwell in them. Woe to the inhabiters of the earth and of the sea! For the devil is come down unto you, having great wrath, because he knoweth that he hath but a short time. And when the dragon saw that he had been cast unto the earth, he persecuted the woman which brought forth the man child.**" *Revelation 12:13*

The *Book of Revelations* not only tells us that Satan will be cast of heaven, but, the answer to the Lord's prayer, will also be accomplished at the same time. With the casting out of Satan, God's will begins to be done on earth as it is in heaven. The *Book of Revelation* also tells us how this will be accomplished. "**And I heard a loud voice saying in heaven, Now is come salvation, and strength, and the kingdom of our God, and the power of his Christ: for the accuser of our brethren is cast down, which accused them before God day and night. And they overcame him by the blood of the Lamb, and by the word of their testimony; and they loved not their**

lives unto the death." *Revelation 12:10-11*

Christians, using their knowledge of the power of Christ's blood, along with their knowledge of the Sword of the Spirit, the word of their testimony, are the ones who cast Satan out of the heavenlies. Author Derek Prince, in his book *Secrets Of A Prayer Warrior,* states: **"They do this using God's atomic weapon: the blood of the Lamb and the word of their testimony. You are probably aware of what is often referred to as 'pleading the blood.' I believe that the majority of Christians have never considered carefully and scripturally what it really means to use the blood of the Lamb by the word of our testimony."** When we have a revelation of what the blood of Jesus has purchased for us, we can then use his name also to enforce Jesus' defeat of Satan in the heavenly realm. After the Manchild is caught up to heaven, the Sun-Clad-Woman is aided by God in her flight as symbolized by the two wings of an eagle. The sign-woman flees into the wilderness where she is protected, thus the Great Red Dragon then goes off to make war with the rest of her seed. **"And when the dragon saw that he was cast unto the earth, he persecuted the women which brought forth the man child. And to the woman were given two wings of a great eagle, that she might fly into the wilderness, into her place, where she is nourished for a time, and times, and half a time, from the face of the serpent."** *Revelation 12:13-14*

To recap, let me say again, the Sun-clad-Woman represents all of God's elect, throughout the dispensations, both *Old Testament*, and *New Testament*, who have resisted Satan in an effort to produce the promised Seed of the Woman. The sign-woman has crown of twelve stars which speaks to both the twelve patriarchs of Israel, and the twelve apostles of the Church. The sign-woman is clothed with the sun which points to Jesus who will come again to complete the redemption of both Israel, and the Church. The moon, which represents all of the powers of darkness throughout both the ancient Babylonian-Pagan world, and the modern New-Age pagan world, is under the sign-woman's feet. This points to the fact that both the *Old Testament*, and *New Testament* saints have gained authority over all the power of the Devil. After leaving Egypt, Israel escaped Pharaoh's Army by passing through the waters. The sign-woman will likewise safely pass through **great eagle, that she might fly into the wilderness, into her place, where she is nourished for a time, and times, and half a time** (three and one half years), **from the face of the serpent. And the serpent cast out of his**

mouth water as a flood after the woman, that he might cause her to be carried away of the flood." *Revelation 12:15*

The sign-woman will quickly flee eastward, out of Jerusalem to the rock hewn city of Sela, or Petra (read my book *The Synagogue of Satan*), which is also known as Bozrah, in Mount Seir. Mount Seir is located near Mount Hor, in the ancient land of Edom and Moab, close to the location where Israel wandered aimlessly for forty years. "Then let them which be in Judaea flee into the mountains (Mount Seir and Mount Hor): Let him which is on the housetop not come down to take anything out of his house: Neither let him which is in the field return back to take his clothes." *Matthew 24:16-18*

The sign-woman supernaturally escapes Satan's grasp for a specific period of time equaling three and a half years, or 1260 days. This period of time represent the last half of the seven-year tribulation period, which is also called the Great Tribulation. When Satan casts water out of his mouth to destroy the sign-woman, the earth opens its mouth and swallowed the flood. "And the serpent cast out of his mouth water as a flood after the woman, that he might cause her to be carried away of the flood. And the earth helped the woman, and the earth opened her mouth, and swallowed up the flood which the dragon cast out of his mouth." *Revelation 12:15-16*

When Satan sees that his efforts to destroy the sign-woman is supernaturally defeated, he is in a rage. Satan then has no recourse other than to turn his destructive efforts towards the remainder of the seed of the woman on earth which faithfully keep, and confess God's Word. "And the dragon was wroth with the woman, and went to make war with the remnant of her seed, which keep the commandments of God, and have the testimony of Jesus Christ." *Revelation 12:17*

The remnant of the Sign-woman's seed are obviously born-again, Bible believing Christians, around the world, who faithfully confess Jesus as their Lord, in the face of persecution. Satan could not stop Jesus, he could not destroy the Sun-Clothed Woman, but he will be successful in making war against the remnant of the sign-woman's seed for three and a half years. "And there was given unto him (the Antichrist) a mouth speaking great things and blasphemies; and power was given unto him to continue forty and two months (three and a half years). And he opened his mouth in blasphemy against God, to blaspheme his name, and his tabernacle, and them that dwell in heaven. And it was given unto him to make war with the saints, and to overcome them: and power was given him over all kindreds, and tongues, and nations. And all that dwell upon the earth shall worship him, whose names are not written in the book of life of the Lamb slain from the foundation of the earth." *Revelation 13:5-8*

"And when he had opened the fifth seal, I saw under the alter the souls of them who were slain for the word of God, and for the testimony which they held.

And they cried with a loud voice, saying, How long, O Lord, holy and true, dost thou not judge and avenge our blood on them that dwell on the earth?

And white robs were given unto every one of them; and it was said unto them, that they should rest yet for a little season, until their fellow-servants also and their brethren, that should be killed as they were, should be fulfilled."

And I beheld when he had opened the sixth seal, and lo, there was a great earthquake; and the sun became black as sackcloth of hair, and the moon became as blood.

And the stars (meteorites) of heaven fell unto the earth, even as a fig tree casteth her untimely figs, when she is shaken of a mighty wind.

And the heaven departed as a scroll when it is rolled together; and every mountain and island were moved out of their places.

And the kings of the earth, and the great men, and the rich men, and the chief captains, and the mighty men, and every bond-man, and every free man, hid themselves in the dens and in the rocks of the mountains;

And said to the mountains and rocks, Fall on us, and hide us from the face of him that sitteth on the throne, and from the wrath of the Lamb:

For the great day of his wrath is come; and who shall be able to stand? *Revelation 6:9-17*

"And at that time shall Michael stand up, the great prince which standeth for the children of thy people: and there shall be a time of trouble, such as never was since there was a nation even to that same time: and at that time thy people shall be delivered, everyone that shall be found written in the book." *Daniel 12:1*

"And I saw an angel (Michael) come down from heaven, having the key of the bottomless pit and a great chain in his hand. And he laid hold on the dragon, that old serpent, which is the Devil, and Satan, and bound him a thousand years. And cast him into the bottomless pit, and shut him up, and set a seal upon him, that he should deceive the nations no more, till the thousand years should be fulfilled: and after that he must be loosed a little season." *Revelation 20:1-3*

Yes it is given unto Satan and his Antichrist to bruise, and make war with the Saints of God for a three and a half years, and to behead multitudes of them. But, the Promised Seed, in death, will overcome Satan's authority over their lives and will ultimately rule and reign with Christ for a thousand years, "And I saw thrones, and they sat upon them, and judgement was given unto them: and I saw the souls of them that were beheaded for the witness of Jesus, and for the word of God, and which had not worshipped the beast (Antichrist), neither his image, neither had received his mark upon their foreheads, or in their hands; and they lived and reigned with Christ a thousand years." *Revelation 20:4*

We, who are living in the last days, will be the ones who, with God's anointing, will be able to stand against all of Satan's traps and snares. At the second coming of Christ, the believing Jews who have fled out to Petra, will see Christ passing over head, on his journey to the Mount of Olives. Pryor to this, Christ will have already attacked Syria, and the armies of the Antichrist, destroying all its terrorists, thus Christs raiment's are covered in blood. Then will be fulfilled the prophecy of Isiah, which states: "Who is this that cometh from Edom, with dyed garments from Bozrah? This that is glorious in his apparel? Traveling in the greatness of his strength? I that speak in rightness, mighty to save. Wherefore art thou red in thine apparel, and thy garments like him that treadeth in the winevat? I have trodden the winepress alone; and of the people there was none with me: for I will tread them in my anger, and trample them in my fury; and their blood shall be sprinkled upon my garments, and I will stain all my raiment. For the day of vengence is in mine heart, and the year of my redeemed is come." *Isaiah 63:1-4*

The Seed of the Woman will surely crush Satan's head and give the victory to all his children. God has not chosen to reveal all things to us at this time, but the *Bible* reveals enough to provide us with the weapons to resist and defeat Satan's plans to steal, kill, and destroy our lives. The Apostle Paul admonished us to be strong in God's word, and use God's armor to defeat the devil. "Finally, my brethren, be strong in the Lord, and in the power of his might. Put on the whole armor of God that ye may be able to stand against the wiles of the Devil. For we wrestle not against flesh and blood, but against principalities, against powers, against the rulers of the darkness of this world, against spiritual wickedness in high places." *Ephesians 6:10-12*

Chapter 14

Victorious Church Vision

Tommy Hicks was an Assemblies of God evangelist who first came to prominence in the 1950s, for his part in the great Argentine Revival. While preaching in Winnipeg Canada, at about 2:30 in the morning, on July 25, 1961, God gave Tommy three consecutive visions in a row. These three visions were not different visions, but rather were all exactly the same in every detail. Tommy had earlier been preaching on the subject of the "Bride of Christ, the Glorious Church, without spot or wrinkle." Christ's bride, the Glorious Church, said Tommy, shall prevail over all the works of the Devil, and nothing, not even the "Gates of Hell," shall prevail against it. In essence, what Tommy was saying was the "Woman's Seed," shall ultimately prevail over the Seed of Satan, as promised in the Garden of Eden. Tommy had earlier been teaching on the traditional Jewish Wedding, and how it related to the Second Coming of Christ. Tommy said: **"The bride longs for her Bridegroom, and will make herself ready for his coming."**

"The Spirit and the bride say, Come" *Revelation 22:17*

Tommy said: this Glorious Church, represented by the Sun-clothed women, and her overcoming-seed, will rise up in the last-days, and, with a great anointing, destroy all the works of the Devil. **"And they overcame him** (the Devil) **by the blood of the Lamb, and by the word of their testimony; and they loved not their lives unto the death."** *Revelation 12:11*

In the traditional ancient Jewish wedding, the father always chose the appropriate bride for his son. The son then had to go to the bride's house, and ask her father for the brides hand in marriage. The Son did not go empty handed, but brought jewels of gold and silver, and a small herd of sheep and goats. This payment was called the *Mohar*, or redemption price, which had to be of sufficient value, as not to offend the bride's father. If the redemption price was thought to be insufficient, the bridegroom could negotiate a favorable redemption price, and make a second trip to the bride's house with the balance. After the bride's father was pleased with the re-demption price, a marriage contract had to be agreed upon by both fami-lies. The Son had to then write out, in his own words, a list of promises he, and his family would agree to perform for the new bride. The father of the bride would then call his family together to review these promises, and if the bride was agreeable, a marriage contract was then signed by both fam-ilies, and the betrothal began. To celebrate the betrothal, the bridegroom would bring a full wine skin of new wine to the father of the bride, and together they would drink the "cup of acceptance." At this point only a cer-tificate of divorce could annul the betrothal. After drinking of the cup, the bride had to make a verbal declaration of commitment to her groom, thus officially sealing the betrothal. The sealing of the betrothal was immediate-ly announced to all by the blowing of the shofar. Before leaving the bride's house, the groom gave more gifts to the bride, then made one final promise to her stating: "I go to my father's house to prepare a bridal chamber, but I will came again, and take you there." **"I go and prepare a place for you. And if I go and prepare a place for you, I will come again, and receive you to myself; that where I am, there ye may be also."** *John 14:2-3*

The bridegroom at this point would then leave the bride's house, and might not return for one to two years. The bride at that point would be-gan to make her white linen bridal gown, and build her hope chest with gifts from all her relatives. The father of the bride would then appoint a messenger to relay messages back and forth between the couple. During this time back at his father's house, the groom began constructing a brid-al chamber known as a *chuppah*, which was usually an addition onto his father's house. Upon completion of the bridal chamber, the father inspect the chamber, while his wife was making preparations for the marriage sup-per, and overseeing the making of the proper wedding garments. Back at the bride's house, the bride's mother prepared several oil lamps, full of oil because it was not unusual for the groom to reappear in the middle of the night to claim his bride. No one, not even the groom knew exactly when he would come to claim his bride. **"But of that day and hour knoweth no man, no, not the angels of heaven, but my father only."** *Matthew 24:36*

"For yourselves knew perfectly that the day of the Lord so cometh as a thief in the night." *I Thessalonians 5:2*

"Then shall the kingdom of heaven be likened unto ten virgins,

which took their lamps, and went forth to meet the bridegroom. And five of them were wise, and five were foolish. They that were foolish took their lamps, and took no oil with them. But the wise took oil in their vessels with their lamps. While the bridegroom tarried, they all slumbered and slept. And at midnight there was a cry made, Behold, the bridegroom cometh; go ye out to meet him. Then all those virgins arose, and trimmed their lamps. And the foolish said unto the wise, Give us of your oil; for our lamps are gone out. But the wise answered, saying, Not so; lest there be not enough for us and you: but go ye rather to them that sell, and buy for yourselves. And while they went to buy, the bridegroom came; and they that were ready went in with him to the marriage: and the door was shut. Afterwards came also the other virgins, saying, Lord, Lord, open to us. But he answered and said, Verily I say unto you, I know you not. Watch therefore, for you know neither the day nor the hour wherein the Son of man cometh." *Matthew 25:1-13*

Tommy went on to describe his vision, saying: "I suddenly found myself at a great height. I was looking down upon the earth, when suddenly the whole world came into view-every nation, every kindred, every tongue came before my sight. From the east and the west; from the north and the south; I recognized the countries and cities that I had been in. I was almost in fear and trembling as I stood beholding the great sight before me. At that moment, when the world came into view, it began to lightning and thunder.

As the lighting flashed over the face of the earth, my eyes went downward-and I was facing the north. Suddenly I beheld what looked like a great giant. As I stared and looked at it, I was almost bewildered by the sight. The giant was gigantic. His feet seemed to reach to the North Pole and his head to the South Pole. His arms were stretched from sea to sea. I could not even begin understand whether this was a mountain or whether this was a giant. As I watched, I suddenly beheld that it was a great giant. I could see he was struggling for life, to even live. His body was covered with debris from head to foot; and at times this great giant would move his body and act as though he would rise up. When he did, thousands of little creatures seemed to run away. Hideous looking creatures would run away from this giant and when he would become calm, they would come back.

All of a sudden this great giant lifted one hand toward the heavens, and then he lifted his other hand. When he did, these creatures by the thousands seemed to flee away from this giant and go out into the night. Suddenly this great giant began to rise-and as he did, his head and hands went into the clouds. As he arose to his feet he seemed to have cleansed himself from the debris and filth that was upon him, and he began and he began to raise his hands into the heavens as though praising the Lord. As he raised his hands, they went even into the clouds.

Suddenly, every cloud became silver; the most beautiful silver that I have ever known. As I watched the phenomenon, it was so great, I could not even began to understand what it all meant. I was so stirred as I watched it. I cried unto the Lord and I said, "Oh, Lord, what is the meaning of this?" And it felt as if I was actually in the spirit and I could feel the presence of the Lord, even as I was asleep.

From those clouds, suddenly there came great drops of liquid light running down upon this mighty giant. Slowly, slowly, this giant began to melt-began to sink, as it were, into the very earth itself. As he melted, his whole form seemed to have melted upon the face of the earth. This great rain began to come down. Liquid drops of light began to flood the very earth itself. As I watched this giant that seemed to melt, suddenly it became millions of people over the face of the earth. As I beheld the sight before me, people stood up all over the world. They were lifting their hands and they were praising the Lord.

At that very moment there came a great thunder that seemed to roar from the heavens. I turned my eyes toward the heavens, and suddenly I saw a figure in white. It glistened, yet somehow I knew that it was the Lord Jesus Christ. He stretched forth his hand. As he did, He would stretch it forth to one, and to another, and to another as He stretched forth His hand upon the peoples and the nations of the world-men and women. As He pointed toward them, this liquid light seemed to flow from His hand into this person and a mighty anointing of God came upon them. Those people began to go forth in the name of the Lord.

I do not know how long I watched it. It seemed it went into days and weeks and months. I beheld this Christ as He continued to stretch forth His hand. But there was a tragedy. There were many people, as He stretched forth His hands, that refused the anointing of God and call of God. I saw men and women that I knew, people that I felt that certainly they would receive the call of God. As He stretched forth His hand toward this one, and toward that one, they simply bowed their heads and began to back away. To each of these that seemed to bow down and back away, they seemed to go into darkness. Blackness seemed to swallow them everywhere.

I was bewildered as I watched it. These people that He had anointed covered the earth. There were hundreds of thousands of these people all over the world--in Africa, Asia, Russia, China, America-all over the world. The anointing of God was upon these people as they went forth in the name of the Lord. I saw these men and women as they went forth. They were ditch diggers, they were washer women, they were rich men, they were poor men. I saw people who were bound with paralysis and sickness, and blindness, and deafness. As the Lord stretched forth His hand to give them this anointing, they became well, they became healed-and they went forth.

This is the miracle of it. This is the glorious miracle if it. Those people would stretch forth their hands exactly as the Lord did, and it seemed that there was this same liquid fire that seemed to be in their hands. According to by word, be thou made whole.

As these people continued in this mighty end-time ministry, I did not fully realize what it was. I looked to the Lord and said, What is the meaning of this? He said, This is that, that I will do in the last day. I will restore all the cankerworm, the palmerworm, the caterpillar – I will restore all that they have destroyed. This, My people in the end-time, shall go forth and as a mighty army shall they sweep over the face of the earth.

As I was at this great height, I could behold the whole world. I watched these people as they were going to and fro over the face of the earth. Suddenly there was a man in Africa, and in a moment he was transported in the Spirit of God, and perhaps he was in Russia, or China, or America, or some other place, and vice versa. All over the world these people went. They came through fire and through pestilence and through famine. Neither fire nor persecution-nothing seemed to stop them.

Angry mobs came to them with swards and with guns, and like Jesus, they passed through the multitude and they could not find them. But they went forth in the name of the Lord. Everywhere they stretched forth their hands, the sick were healed, the blind eyes were opened. There was not a long prayer. I never saw a church, and I never saw or heard a denomination. These people were going in the name of the Lord of Hosts.

As they marched forward as the ministry of Christ in the end-time, these people ministered to the multitudes over the face of the earth. Tens of thousands, even millions seemed to come to the Lord Jesus Christ as these people stood forth and gave the message of the kingdom-of the coming kingdom-in the last hour. It was so glorious! It seemed there were those that rebelled. They would become angry. They tried to attack those workers that were giving the message.

God is going to give to the world a demonstration in this last hour such as the world has never known. These men and women are of all walks of life. Degrees will mean nothing. I saw these workers as they were going over the face of the earth. When one would seem to stumble and fall, another would come and pick him up. There were no big I, or little you. Every mountain was brought low and every valley was exalted.

They seemed to have one thing in common. There was a divine love that seemed to flow forth from these people, as they went together, as they worked together, as they lived together. It was the theme of their life. They continued and it seemed the days went by as I stood and beheld this sight. I could only cry-and sometimes I laughed. It was so wonderful as these people went throughout the face of the whole earth showing forth God's power in this last end-time.

As I watched from the very heaven itself, there were times when great deluges of this liquid light seemed to fall upon great congregations. The congregations would lift their hands and seemingly praise God for hours and even days, as the Spirit of God came upon them. God said, I will pour out my spirit upon all flesh. That is exactly the thing that God was doing. From every man and woman that received this power and the anointing of God, the miracles of God flowed continuously.

Suddenly there was another great clap of thunder that seemed to re-sound around the world. Again I heard the voice saying: "Now this is my people; this is my beloved bride." When the voice spoke, I looked upon the earth and I could see the lakes and the mountains. The graves were opened and people from all over the world, the saints of all ages, seemed to be rising. As they rose from the graves-suddenly all these people came from every direction-from the east and the west, from the north and the south. They seemed to be forming again into this gigantic body. As the dead in Christ seemed to be rising first, I could hardly comprehend it. It was so marvelous. It was so far beyond anything I could ever dream or think of.

This huge body suddenly began to form and take shape again, and its shape was in the form of the mighty giant,, but this time it was different. It was arrayed in the most beautiful, gorgeous white. Its garments were without spot or wrinkle as this body began to form. And the people of all ages seemed to be gathering into this body. Slowly, from the heavens above, the Lord Jesus came and became the head. I heard another clap of thunder that said: "This is my beloved bride for whom I have waited. She will come forth, even tried by fire. This is she that I have loved from the beginning of time." As I watched, my eyes turned to the far north and I saw great destruction, men and women in anguish and crying out, and buildings destroyed. Then I heard again, the fourth voice that said: "Now is my wrath being powered out upon the face of the earth." From the ends of the whole world, it seemed that there were great vials of God's wrath being poured out upon the face of the earth. I can remember it as I beheld the awful sight of seeing the cities, and whole nations going down into destruction. I could hear the weeping and the wailing. I could hear people crying. They seemed to cry as they went into caves, but the caves and the mountains opened up. They leaped into water, but the water would not drown them. There was nothing that seemingly could destroy them. They were wanting to take their lives but they did not succeed.

Again I turned my eyes toward the glorious sight of this body arrayed in the beautiful white shining garment. Slowly, slowly, it began to lift from the earth, and as it did, I awoke. This sight that I had beheld-I had seen the end-of-time ministry, the last hour." Tommy Hicks was privileged to get a glimpse of the last-day victorious Church, promised by God, all the way back in the Garden of Eden. "And I will put enmity between thee (Satan) and the women, and between thy seed and her seed; it shall bruise thy head, and thou shalt bruise his heel." *Genesis 3:15*

Christ, the victorious second Adam, will in the end, receive his new glorious Eve, without spot or wrinkle, the victorious Church. Together, after crushing the head of Satan, they both will reign side by side for an eternity.

www.ingramcontent.com/pod-product-compliance
Lightning Source LLC
Chambersburg PA
CBHW071440090426
42737CB00011B/1732